NATIVE STORY BASED IN KENYA

Extreme Odds

ENDURED

| EFFIE | RUBIA |

Journey through the life of Almasi and explore how a second wife and mother's love can overcome all things.

Copyright © 2023 Effie Rubia

Publishing services by Krystal Lee Enterprises LLC (KLE Publishing)

All rights reserved. No parts of this book may be reproduced, distributed, or used in any manner, including photocopying, recording, or other electronic or mechanical methods without the prior written permission of the copywriter owner, except for the use of brief quotations in a book review and certain noncommercial uses permitted by copyright law.

Print: 978-1-945066-38-2
E-book: 978-1-945066-40-5

Paperback:
All rights reserved. Please send comments and questions:
Krystal Lee Enterprises
sales@KLEPub.com

To Reach the Author:
Web: EffieRubia.com / IG: @effierubia
FB: Effie Rubia   Email: emuboka@yahoo.com

Printed in the United States of America.
Disclaimers
The information in this book was correct at the time of publication, but the Author does not assume any liability for loss or damage caused by errors or omissions. These are my memories, from my perspective, and I have tried to represent events as faithfully as

possible where necessary.

Dedication

This book is affectionately dedicated to My Mother, for always loving and supporting me. You did not go away, but walked beside me every day. You are unseen, unheard, but always near. So loved you are and missed very dearly.

Chapters

Chapter 1	7
Chapter 2	17
Chapter 3	33
Chapter 4	37
Chapter 5	47
Chapter 6	63
Chapter 7	79
Chapter 8	89
Chapter 9	99
Chapter 10	105
Chapter 11	111
Chapter 12	127
Chapter 13	131
Chapter 14	143
Chapter 15	163
Chapter 16	173
Chapter 17	177
About the Author	183

Chapter 1 – Mother

"No matter what struggles I come across, I will keep going because I have the will and strength to overcome it all. All my greatest accomplishments I once thought I would never achieve, but I keep on succeeding every challenge that faces me. No matter what is beyond my control, nothing will ever make me less than a woman. I am and will always be a powerful woman."
~ Victoria Enriquez

Nothing compares to a mother's love for her children. Motherhood comes naturally to most women. Women carry their children until they are born, then love and care for them until adulthood. Every mother ensures that their child is protected and happy throughout their childhood through to adulthood. Only a mother can truly understand what that truly means.

A mother's love for her children fuels these

Chapter 1

emotions. No one can put into words the love a mother has for her children. In reality, oftentimes children do not realize it until they become mothers. Their love always cheers us on when we tumble down in life. Mothers are the only ones who do not have demands other than what is in the best interest for her children's future.

A mother's love for her children cannot and will not be measured up to anything. It is a pure form of love which is impossible to explain. Our mothers are more lenient than anyone we have or will ever meet. They forgive us even when we have immensely wronged them. A mother's degree of mercy is unrivaled. They overlook our mistakes and still love us. This unique connection between mother and child who bears all things. It is a bond that is reliable and veritable till the very end.

Hi, my name is Euphemia by the way. I realized I started talking before introducing myself. My mother, Almasi, was born in a small-town village in Kenya. She was the third child born of a family of four. The town she grew up in wasn't like a typical African village. It wasn't easy to get things done. Almasi's family struggled to get food, work, clothes, and anything—even going to school was difficult.

No matter the difficulties, her parents sacrificed that she could go to school. Almasi did just that; she went to school and performed very well.

She didn't let her parents down as she knew how hard they worked for her success. Almasi became the first lady, and the first child from the village to attend high school and go on through to college. She accomplished things nobody in the town had ever done.

Graduating college meant looking for her first job and that job required her to move to the city. Almasi had to move from her hometown to Nairobi. Almasi's life in the village was harsh and unbearable for so many. She once told her daughter, Euphemia, they were so deep in a crisis that her family couldn't afford clothes. Almasi would retell incidents to her daughter of how she only had only two dresses, and those clothes were torn.

Almasi had to wear the torn dress whenever she visited the market. SheWhenhe would turn around in embarrassment whenever someone passed by her, hiding the hole in her dress. After they had gone, she would turn back around. As Almasi told these stories to her daughter she often broke out laughing just remembering what it was like and how God brought her through made her thankful. Clothes were not the only challenge for Almasi's parents, food also was scarce. Balancing education with everyday needs took sacrifice. Eating once a day became normal and it is highly possible she was malnourished all her young life. Her parents gave their best, but what can you do when you give your

Chapter 1

best and it is not enough? Eating once a day was not enough, but had to make it due and she survived.

There was an entirely different path her life took when she moved to the city for her job. The best thing that could have been given to her was education. When graduating from college with her degree as a secretary, she got a job in one of the large companies in Nairobi n. There she worked as a secretary to the manager of the largest brewery company in Kenya at the time.

Everything was different for her when she first arrived in the city. The lights, housing, and even the air seemed different. Almasi had never gone to the city as a child growing up; it was her first time living in such a busy city. Her ordinary life in the village did not prepare her at all for entering this busy big world. She didn't know how to drive, the cultural norms, or how to get around the city.

Nonetheless, Almasi was a woman who never gave up and would rise to any occasion. She learned how to drive and got herself a driving license within a few weeks. As time went by, Almasi enjoyed working in the brewery company. Of course, it started off with challenges and the realization that what you learn in college doesn't always prepare you for the job.

She would often tell her children it was one of the

best places she had ever worked. This was not a lie, but the result was intentional. She loved talking about her experiences with her children—especially with her daughter, Euphemia.

Time passed, and her life moved on. While working at the company, Almasi befriended many people. Among them was a young handsome man named Luca, who adored her. The more time they spent together, gradually changed their friendly companionship to love.

Almasi and Luca started dating and things took off for them quickly. She was in love, but unsure how she felt about remaining in a serious relationship so quickly heading towards what seemed like a lifetime commitment. She was sure of her feelings but not too sure he was the "one." She thought she had time to process her thoughts because the relationship was still fairly new, but in Luca's heart, the next step was now.

When he proposed, Almasi went into her most feared dilemma. She had to decide to be true to her feelings and honest with Luca. Or to spare him of any potential pain and say, "YYes." After much thought, not knowing what to say because she did not want to break his heart, she settled on a decision hesitantly. Almasi decided to turn him down after realizing she was not ready to commit.

Chapter 1

Although she felt great about being honest, it broke Luca's heart. The unthinkable happened, she got the news he committed suicide. It was a deep hit to her heart. She had never thought her truth could cause so much damage to someone else's life. His death was a shock. Almasi never could've imagined that he would kill himself. It was an adamant time for her. Her first love had taken his life because of her feelings . For months, the guilt and anguish didn't let her live peacefully. She would wake up in the night, horrified and troubled. Not only did she break his heart but broke his life. The nightmares wouldn't make her life easier either.

Almasi never wanted to talk about it to her children. It was an unfortunate incident that she wanted to forget but found it hard to. Regardless, one day, when she was doing laundry with Euphemia, Almasi told her daughter,

"Someone was in love with me once, and we were in a relationship…"

"What happened then, Mom?" Little Euphemia asked her mother.

"He asked me to marry him, but I refused his hand in marriage ." Almasi hesitated to tell her daughter the truth. Luca's face turned up in her mind.

"Then?"

"Luca couldn't take it," Almasi sighed. "He ended up committing suicide."

It took a while for Almasi before she got into another relationship. She couldn't get over the stigma behind it. However, the next person she fell in love with turned from groom to gloom to doom. Barasa was from a very wealthy family inKenya. At the time, this country was one of the countries colonized by the British, and as such, the villages had chiefs as leaders.. Barasa's father was one of the chiefs of his village.

Barasa is from the Bukusu tribe. Bukusu are one of the Kenyan clans of the East African Luhya Bantu people. They mostly lived in Bungoma and Trans Nzoia counties. They share ancestors with the Luhya and the Gisu of Uganda.. Bukusu tribe–who call themselves BaBukusu–is the most prominent clan of the Luhya nation, accounting for approximately thirty-four percent of the population. They communicate in the Bukusu dialect primarily.

Almasi and Barasa had a chance meeting in Nairobi. He was there to visit his brother–one of the ministers–in the 70s. He wasn't a well-known leader but had his own level of influence. Soon, they fell in love and started dating. Almasi was on cloud nine because she felt blessed to meet Barasa. However, the

Chapter 1

truth was far too horrid. Barasa didn't disclose he had another family. It only became evident when their relationship had grown into marriage, and there was no going back for her after that..

Almasi's life turned upside down when she learned her new husband was polygamous. Polygamy in the Bukusu tribe is common and nothing new to the people growing up in the tribes in Africa, and Kenya is not excluded. And for that reason, Almasi just ended up getting married to him.

Barasa's family after several years of not having a baby, stopped embracing her because, in their eyes, she was a failure . They treated her differently and they kept it secret that Barasa was looking for another wife. Loyalty to Almasi from Barasa's family withdrew . She was betrayed by her lover and in-laws. This was tough for her. Since Barasa already had a wife, Almasi was his second wife with no clear direction.

Almasi didn't lose faith in her value nor in the idea there was a purpose for her life. She still loved her husband, even though he began mistreating her. She would help her husband and do anything for him or his family. - She was earning good money and was able to take care of herself, Barasa, and his family. Everything Almasi did was looked down upon, however. It was as if her hard work wass up to 'no good.' Barasa never acknowledged her love and care the way she deserved.

All Barasa wanted was a third wife' for the sole purpose of having children for him. Children are considered a sign of wealth in the Bukusu tribe, it is no mystery as to why Almasi was not valuable in his culture. i In the village, money was not everything, but here what was powerful currency and prestige was children and she didn't have that. Almasi was not able to have children for ten years. It resulted in Barasa, her husband, going ahead and marrying again.

The new wife ended up having children quickly. Meanwhile, Almasi still couldn't get pregnant. It was such a devastating period in her lifetime. She was taunted and became a laughingstock within her family. She prayed and fasted so many times she would cry herself to sleep praying that God could bless her with children. All this while Almasi was caring for Barasa's other children from the third wife. She lived with some of her stepchildren, cared for all their needs, and even took them to very good schools and paid their tuition.

It wasn't until the second wife gave birth to three children before Almasi gave birth to Euphemia. After that, Almasi gave birth to four more children, Baraka, then the twins, Ezra and Ivy, and the youngest, Zion.

Chapter 1

She thought giving her husband children would change him, it did not happen as she expected. Life wasn't easy for Almasi; what she visualized as a blessing turned into a disaster and torture. The family tried their hardest to break her resolve. Almasi had not had an easy childhood, so she built resilience, and no one was going to let break her.

But! She had endurance that could not crack a camel's back. Even after bearing so much trouble, she didn't let anyone stop her from fighting for her life and the children she had been blessed with. Almasi was already determined and independent, however, her children gave her more reason to fight.

Chapter 2 – Growing up in an unhealthy Environment

"No matter what you've suffered, the abuse was not your fault. Not as an innocent child, teenager, nor as an adult."
~Dana Arcuri

A family is among the most valuable gifts God has bestowed upon us. It is a blessing to have a healthy relationship with family, as not everybody has it. It is pure joy to have parents and siblings that love you. Family members are a shield t God had put in place to surround and guard you from imminent dangers that roam around looking to destroy.

However, for Euphemia, it was different. A polygamous family was the least of her wishes or dreams. Euphemia believed polygamy was never good, and as she would say, it was not anything appealing–especially from a child's perspective. She observed she was no longer the

Chapter 2

center of attention from two individuals–a father and a mother. It now involved a second, third, fourth, fifth, and even sixth mother, of whom did not give birth to her, nor treat her as their own child. Stepparenting normally includes these natural instincts for forming family bonds with children outside their current relationship.

What do you do when the outside and present relationship are both happening at the same time? It was complicated for Euphemia to understand precisely why this could happen. She grappled with the reasons behind polygamy. To her as a child it never made sense, especially at times when favoritism existed between her and her step-siblings. It was worse when Euphemia and her siblings saw their mother's being mistreated by their father. Polygamy became a horrendous experience for children oftentimes.

The Bible says that committing adultery is wrong, and a relationship between a man and a woman that is sacred. Euphemia would often think of the logistics, wouldn't he have to date another woman while married to another? If so, isn't adultery committed at that point? It never made any sense to the young Euphemia. It was all a heartache to her because no one looked happy, not even her father. In ninety percent of polygammous families, cheating happened in the marriage, resulting in one person marrying another; it seemed wrong to her.

It wasn't only the 'polygamy' factor that disturbed her but the mistreatment and discrimination she and her siblings faced throughout their life. Euphemia wanted the love and care of her parents like any normal child. She wanted her family to be like a normal family; however, what she got instead was fear, pain, and suffering.

***

"I told you to listen to me!" Barasa shouted, kicking Almasi.

He moved away from his wife, who was lying injured and assaulted on the ground. Her hair was tousled and dirty. Her lips were split, and her eyes had tears in them. Almasi's arms and legs had ugly marks and spots from the beating.

Euphemia and Baraka gasped, peeking behind the door, looking at the violent sight. Angry tears flowed from their eyes as they helplessly stood by. They were horrified and disgusted as they saw the aftermath for the first time of their father beating their mother.

How long has it been going on? Euphemia thought. And why doesn't Mum fight back? How can someone be this brutal to his wife?

The siblings were appalled, angry, and frustrated. They felt helpless as they knew they could not do anything to help their mother.

"E-Euphemia…," Baraka stammered but stopped. He didn't know how to word his feelings.

"Shhh!" Euphemia shushed him before Barasa could find them out. "I know what you are thinking…but we…we can't."

Chapter 2

They both went silent after that and watched Almasi. Euphemia and Baraka's eyes widened when they heard their younger siblings calling out for them. Oh, no! Euphemia thought. We need to move before the kids find out about this. Alerted and anxious, they both leaned back and closed the door. Hiding their siblings from the reality of the cruel world.

It wasn't the only time the siblings saw their father abusing their mother. Barasa made it a habit to violate and insult Almasi. What Euphemia and her brother were unable to understand was why their mother never defended herself. What was she so afraid of?

No matter how much Euphemia thought about it, she would come empty-handed. And one day, she decided it was enough. She had to ask her mother the reason behind all of this.

"Mum," she started saying. "C-can I ask you s-something?"

"What is it, darling?" Almasi asked her. She hadn't seen her daughter stuttering or getting nervous before. It worried her.

"Mum, why…why does dad beat you so bad like that?"

"What?" Almasi was shocked. She wasn't aware her children saw her getting abused. "How…how do you…no, when did you find out?"

"A month ago." Euphemia paused. "Baraka and I saw him slapping and punching you."

"Oh, my darling." Her mother began crying, and immediately, Euphemia ran toward her. She embraced her mother, sobbing along with her. For an hour, the mother-daughter duo wept.

Pained. Hurt.

"Mum," Euphemia uttered, leaning back from the hug. "Please tell me, Mum."

"I don't know." Almasi hiccupped. "I don't really know why he does that."

As Euphemia grew up, she began to understand the reason behind his father's misconduct. She realized he didn't like to see her mother working and wanted her to stop. However, Almasi was a proactive woman. She would run around errands that kept her house and children fed, well dressed and looking good and apparently that made him jealous.

If she wanted to buy cattle, she would buy it herself. If she wanted to do anything, she did it without looking and waiting on him. Such independence displeased him. Almasi didn't need anyone to run her home; she was independent. Euphemia realized her father somehow felt intimidated by her mother's independence.

One day, Barasa sauntered into their house, shouting and throwing insults. Almasi was at work at

Chapter 2

that time, leaving only the children and house workers. Euphemia and Baraka were terrified; they immediately ran into the living room. It's a good thing the kids are sleeping now, Euphemia thought, sighing in relief.

They both just stood there in the living room, staring at their father cursing, grumbling, and pacing like a mad person. His voice was so loud that they could not hear what he said. The second his eyes fell on the pictures on the wall, Barasa's expression turned dark. It was as if a devil entered inside him.

Swiftly, Euphemia watched her father moving toward the pictures. He glared at the photographs and snatched them from the wall. Enraged, Barasa threw them on the floor. The picture frames shattered into tiny pieces. Euphemia and Baraka jumped in fright, some of the pieces falling at their feet as they were barefoot.

"Don't...don't do it," Euphemia and Baraka pleaded, crying continuously. When their father didn't acknowledge them, they uttered, "Please, don't do it."

Furious, Barasa turned toward them and grunted, "You have not cried yet!"

"W-w-what?" Euphemia stammered.

"You both have not cried yet!" Barasa laughed wickedly. "You are yet to cry, and I promise I will make sure of it."

After uttering those words, he walked out of the

house and drove off.

***

Euphemia had a loving relationship with her mother and siblings. They cared for one another as any other family would. However, Euphemia and her siblings had a broken relationship with their step brothers and sisters. They never conversed with each other, played together, but they were aware of one another. For a time she wanted a relationship, but any time her step-siblings would reach out, it was mainly pretentious.

Euphemia and her younger siblings had no other choice but to go with the flow. They never fought back or retorted to their step-sibling's. It was mainly because they didn't have any other family support besides their mother. Barasa only supported and loved his first and third wife and their children—as if Almasi, Euphemia, Baraka, Ezra, Ivy, and Zion never existed or were a priority.

Euphemia believed favoritism and jealousy were not good for a healthy relationship. Her family never confronted anyone about it but would hush the comments and thoughts from lingering in the air. Masked relationships were evident in polygamous families among the mothers and siblings.

As they grew older and matured enough, Euphemia and her sibling's allowed themselves to think open-mindedly. They just forged direct relationships–not really strong–but where they could just get along with their extended family. They would behave to their step-relatives like any other extended family—agreeing

Chapter 2

on some things and disagreeing on others.

Barasa continued to show discrimination; he was nice to Euphemia's step-sisters but not to her. When it came to her and Baraka, he did not care for either of them. Euphemia felt low and neglected every time this happened. She was unable to understand why her father didn't like them.

Did I do something to him, she thought one day, sitting in her room, crying in a corner. "Why does father treat us like this? Are we not his children? Why does he not love us?" she asked herself out loud. It wasn't the first time she had to ponder on this. No, she would, again and again, question her existence.

Barasa ensured Euphemia's step-siblings were better dressed. He didn't buy clothes and food for Euphemia or her family. He would rather leave them starving than provide food on their table. It disturbed Euphemia to see her family being neglected.

Almasi paid school fees for her children as Barasa never bothered. However, he had the audacity to order her around. He would tell her t if she wanted her kids to stay in the private school, then she had to pay school fees for all the other children too!

Barasa would pick up and drop Euphemia's step-siblings from school and take them to their home. Meanwhile, Almasi's children had to take public transportation to and from school.

***

Almasi sacrificed to take her children to good private boarding schools. The schools had three terms a year. Every time school opened and closed, Almasi could only afford to drop-off and pick-up her children at the beginning and end of the term using public transportation. The school had midterm breaks, where they closed the school. It was always so exciting for her to go back home and see her mother and siblings, even for just one month.

Along with her siblings, they stayed home for almost two months for Christmas breaks. She enjoyed the time she spent with her family. It was the most beautiful time of her life. However, whenever it was time to go back to school, it was never easy for them, especially for Euphemia. She didn't want to leave her mom alone. She wasn't sure if she would see her mother again. Euphemia feared if her mother would be safe from her father's wrath. She knew her father would sometimes get abusive.

Euphemia never knew whether her family would come to a place they called home when they came back from school. Even as years passed, her father's harsh words kept resonating in her mind. "You will leave this house! Do you listen to me? Whether you like it or not. You will have to leave this house!" Barasa had shouted at her mother one day.

Euphemia and her siblings never understood why Barasa wanted them out of that home. But they later learned that apparently, he had promised to give their home and land to one of his wives. Euphemia didn't know if her father was pressured to act that way or if it was his

Chapter 2

own decision. And to this day, she still had no idea what all that was.

When it was time to go back to school, the only thing that Euphemia was excited about was being bought new stuff. New uniforms and the different snacks her mother would bring her and her siblings to carry to school. The children could eat it of their own will, anytime they wanted to. It was exciting for them. It wasn't like Almasi couldn't provide those snacks to them at home because she knew they would gobble down everything if given the opportunity. She had strict rules on snacks when they were at home.

Euphemia being the oldest took responsibility for looking after her younger siblings. Almasi was a working woman; she had to leave for work early in the morning—before the children could even wake up and return late in the evening. Euphemia shouldered several chores assisted by house workers and sometimes her cousins from her mother's side. Whenever Almasi was at home, she would teach her daughter how to be responsible and caring. Euphemia was the 'mother' figure to her siblings. She would ensure her siblings' school bags were packed.

Euphemia saw her mother requesting to take a lift from the Newspaper vehicle drivers whenever she was late. She felt relieved knowing her mother got there faster, fairly comfortable and efficient. She knew Almasi would always be on time to work as she didn't take public transport vehicles that usually stopped at every town to pick passengers and goods.

My mother was always comfortable taking the

newspaper vehicles though sometimes fearful of the speed at which they were driven. And for Almasi it was a rather confident way of knowing her children got to work safely when she saw the newspaper vehicle. Almasi had to work during the week, so Euphemia and her siblings went to school on their own by public transport, or a cousin would drop them to school. Almasi was an extraordinary human being. She was a risk-taker but in a good and responsible way.

Euphemia knew her mother was fearless. However, most of the time, Almasi would hike a newspaper vehicle to drop her children off to school as they dropped the newspapers along the way to different towns. During those years Kenya had only two Newspaper companies that distributed newspapers; Nation and Standard. They both published newspapers only in Nairobi. The publication of the papers was completed at midnight and distributed through the night till the morning.

To circulate the papers around the town early, the drivers drove very fast but carefully. It wasn't easy for Euphemia at first. She was hesitant to travel in those vans as she thought of all the vehicle accidents. They all were due to either reckless driving, unstructured roads, or drunk driving. Every time she traveled with them, Euphemia got anxious about the speed at which the drivers drove the vans. She clutched the seat tightly with one hand, and from the other, she protected her siblings, so she thought.

And after she had safely reached the school, Euphemia thanked God for protecting her and her siblings. Euphemia remembered how busy and frightful it was to

Chapter 2

go to school. She noticed how the highways were jam-packed as both the boarding and day school timings were the same. Looking out of the window, Euphemia gazed at the private and public transportation.

It's so busy she thought, sighing. I hope we don't get into an accident.

A few months ago, accidents kept happening on the highway, where drivers drove at dangerous speeds. However, every time it resulted in fatal accidents. During those days, many children never made it to school. Some ended up dead due to the injuries sustained in road accidents. The accidents made Euphemia more fearful.

Euphemia always prayed and hoped to never come across any traffic accidents anytime she traveled. However, on Kenyan roads that can be somehow inevitable. Many accidents litter the streets because people are in such a hurry.

On this day as children prepared to go back to school, a horrific accident happened just one mile down from Euphemia's house. She heard neighbors in the community talking about it. When she heard about it, she got curious. Instead of continuing to prepare for school, Euphemia followed the crowd.

The moment she arrived at the scene, she couldn't help but frown at the sight. It was sorrowful and disturbing. For a minute, she went numb, as her heart went out to people who had lost their lives and their families. When she came to her senses, Euphemia found out what had actually happened.

She learned that a matatu was carrying passengers of all ages, suitcases (sanduku) and goods some passengers were ferrying to the market. The matatu was traveling in the opposite direction with a truck beside it. Apparently, they both were engaging on the curvy corner, and unexpectedly, one of the drivers' lost their balance and crossed into the other lane. The truck hit the matatu and ripped off almost half the top.

Tangled blood covered bodies, belongings of the deceased, fruits and school books, broken glass windows, and bent vehicle metal were scattered on the black tarmac road. The smell of the blood mixed with the oranges surrounded the environment. It was such a horrifying scene that would end up being embedded into little Euphemia's mind for a long time in her life. After that day, the Aroma from oranges was always a reminder of the scenes of that horrific accident.

Even after years passed by, Euphemia couldn't forget the scene. It was as if it had engraved itself into her mind. She dreaded going to school, especially on opening days, and whenever she had to because that fear would creep in. For years, she remained frightened to drive a car or even travel on the roads. Euphemia believed that her family was blessed; and they were always protected from any incident. She couldn't help but be grateful for God's mercy.

***

Almasi taught Euphemia and her children to be

Chapter 2

responsible and caring people. Not just for others but also for themselves. She wanted her daughter to be as accountable as she was, and Euphemia followed her mother. She would see her mother waking up every morning, taking a shower, and getting dressed. Almasi would dress up elegantly and formally to work. While on the weekends, she dressed casually to do chores. For her children, they were not exempted from doing the same.

Almasi ensured the house workers woke up early, bathed, and dressed her children neatly every day. When Euphemia was in Nursery and lower primary school, her mother dressed them up in neat clothes, socks and shoes –even if they were staying at home.

"Why am I wearing the same socks and shoes in every picture, Mum?" Euphemia asked her mother one day, flipping through the photo album. She was confused as to why every picture of her was almost the same.

Almasi laughed and patted her daughter's back. "I don't know that either," Almasi told her, beaming.

"Huh? What, why?" Euphemia raised an eyebrow in question, getting even more confused.
"I would go to work, leaving you dressed up in socks and shoes. And when I would come back, you would still be in the same shoes and socks."

"Oh!" Euphemia blinked, dumbfounded.

"Also, not only that, I remember how you were fond of reading books. So, I bought books for you." Her mother turned toward her and shook her head, chuckling.

Oh, it looks like I did more embarrassing things than I could think of. Euphemia thought.

"But you never read those books like others. In fact, you would hide under the big round dining table and read under it."

"No way!" Euphemia replied. A second passed by, and the duo burst out laughing. The older woman was amused at her daughter's cuteness, while the young girl was embarrassed.

Even though she didn't have a perfect life, Euphemia was thankful to have a loving and caring family—her mother and siblings. She knew she couldn't have asked for anything better than that.

My childhood, so she built resilience, and no one was going to let break her. She had endurance that could not crack a camel's back. Even after bearing so much trouble, she didn't let anyone stop her from fighting for her life and the children she had been blessed with. Almasi was already determined and independent, however, her children gave her more reason to fight.

Chapter 2

Chapter 3 – The Power of a Praying Mother

"But what is this fear of the Lord? It is that affectionate reverence, by which the child of God bends himself humbly and carefully to his Father's law."
~Charles Bridges

Since Euphemia was little, she watched her mother worship God. She would pray a lot and read the Bible every day. She wanted to instill the fear of God in her children's life. Not in a threatening way but only so that they could worship Him. Almasi ensured she took them to the church and taught them how to pray and tithe.

Euphemia never understood why her mother gave each of her children some coins every Sunday to put in the church baskets. She didn't know the concept behind it and would be left confused. However, as she grew older,

Chapter 3

she understood why her mother taught her the idea of tithing, or really giving. Even though it was not the actual true meaning of tithing as mentioned in the Bible.

Nonetheless, as Euphemia grew older and years passed, she and her siblings understand Christianity, salvation, prayer, and everything. Almasi acknowledged they wanted them to learn more. She bought each of them a bible to help them understand the teachings of God. Euphemia saw her mother underline scripture verses in her Bible. As Almasi continued her daughter's salvation grew, Euphemia learned to do the same.

Euphemia's mother prayed often, and even in tough times, she found solace in prayer. She would occasionally have pastors and preachers come home to pray for her family. Especially when her children would get sick or when they were leaving for school and sometimes when they came home from boarding school for holidays.

Euphemia did not doubt her mother's knowledge, love, serving, and praying to God changed her children's life trajectory. She could say she would not be alive today if it were not for her mother constantly praying for her.

***

One day, Almasi sent Euphemia to town to get some groceries;. As it was far, Euphemia had to take public transportation. It was after she had finished primary school and was waiting to get into high school.

When she was returning from shopping, the vehicle she was using lost its front tire. The driver lost control and the vehicle drifted across someone's farm along the road. Everyone in the car began screaming as the car sped toward a huge tree. Euphemia thought she wouldn't be able to see a new day, that it was her last moment on Earth. Nevertheless, something miraculous happened.

Something no one could comprehend! Suddenly one of the men in the car said almost like screaming in a loud and firm voice "Jesus!" And right then in a flash just before the vehicle would have hit a very huge tree— literally a few inches—the car came to a halt. Everyone was scared but we all scampered out of the vehicle with a sigh of relief. They were still , in a daze, Euphemia heard everyone besides her mumbling, "Thank God!"

It was then that she was relieved, always remembering and knowing her mother was always praying for her. She was sure that mother's prayers had something to do with her not having been involved in a grisly car accident that day.

***

Anyway, as life went on routinely, Euphemia as always saw Almasi reading her Bible and praying before bedtime. Whenever Euphemia was alone with her she would sit with her mother on her mother's bed. The two happily sat facing a large glass window and looking out to the gate. She had always treasured those moments as she and her mother would watch their cattle return from grazing with the herd's boy.

That day Almasi had opened the Bible as usual

Chapter 3

and was silently reading as Euphemia sat there quietly gazing outside. Then all of a sudden, Almasi started praying loudly. Euphemia was confused about what had just happened; she couldn't decipher her mother's sudden reaction.

Before Euphemia could ask her mother what happened, Almasi began talking in a different language, as if she tuned out at that time. Little did Euphemia understand that her mother was speaking in dialects (other tongues). She was frantic, and Euphemia began worrying about her mother's well-being.

"Mom! Mom!" Euphemia shouted. "Are you okay?"

Almasi instantly stopped praying, and glancing at her daughter then, gave her a reassuring smile. After Euphemia had grown up and understood what her mother was doing, she felt terrible for stopping her mother from talking to God. Later, she understood the Holy Spirit was in control at that time. She understood better what that meant soon after, and how being a saved child from death to life gave you gifts to utter things never heard but by anyone but God. I enjoyed being a God-fearing child.

On many occasions, Euphemia and her siblings would see their mother scribbling on a piece of paper in her Bible. Almasi was particularly good at using a diary and even gave her oldest daughter a diary, who was in high school at that time. Numerous times, Euphemia had the privilege of experiencing the power of a praying mother. Her mother not only prayed to God, but also feared Him and instilled the love for God in her children.

Chapter 4 – College

"No matter what struggles I come across, I will keep going because I have the will and strength to overcome it all. All my greatest accomplishments I once thought I would never achieve, but I keep on succeeding every challenge that faces me. No matter what is beyond my control, nothing will ever make me less than a woman. I am and will always be a powerful woman."
~ Victoria Enriquez

In life, we require physical, mental, and emotional effort to go through our different phases. Very few people have things planned out for themselves. Some people are born into wealth, the fortunate ones; however, most people work incredibly hard from the beginning to achieve their goals. For Euphemia, things were different, her mother had wealth but she had to work just as hard as someone who had nothing to overcome the added weight and challenges in her life.

Chapter 4

***

As Euphemia grew up, Barasa stopped abusing Almasi— physically—but the verbal abuse continued. There wasn't a time when he didn't seek an opportunity to insult or taunt her. Even the simplest matters could turn into an argument and he could create havoc. It upset Euphemia that her mother wouldn't stop him. Every time Euphemia wanted to speak up for her mother, Almasi would quiet her down.

"Why?" Euphemia would ask her mother in frustration.

"He is your father, darling," Almasi would answer her with a soft smile on her face.

After time, she comprehended that her mother still cared for her father because he was her children's father. Even though he degraded and showed little to no affection toward her, Almasi cared for her husband. This was something Euphemia never could understand, she thought, how could she love someone who treated her so badly?

***

One day, when Almasi and Euphemia were working in the compound, a tall and masculine man visited. He was well dressed and adorned in multicolored regalia. Euphemia had never seen someone dressed like that in her town. Who is he? she thought, gazing at him. The man had a demeanor you would think he was a king or prince. There were several stars on his regalia like a military sergeant. In tow, he had ten or so immaculately dressed men and women, all in white.

"Hello," Almasi greeted them. "Can I help you?"
"I am Jehova Wanyonyi," the well dressed man introduced himself. "And these are the "Israelites," he exclaimed in confidence.

"Alright," Almasi uttered, weirded out. "Who… who are you?" dumb struck, she could hardly speak. Blasphemy she thought!

"Huh…You don't know me?" Almasi shook her head in denial. No I do not, she replied "I am the God of the lost Israelites, and your husband has been gracious enough to allow us to stay in your land." He looked around, beaming. "This is the promised land."

Euphemia blinked while Almasi stared at him, flabbergasted.

Being a staunch Christian, this was blasphemy for Euphemia and her mother. However, as it was Barasa's decision, they remained quiet. It was rumored that the 'Lost Israelites' had sold all their earthly wealth and gave the proceeds to Jehova Wanyonyi—their 'God'—for blessings. These guys revered him with awe and worshiped him.

Jehova Wanyonyi had a complete marching band that would entertain visitors who came from far and wide just to see who this guy really was. Once in a while, Euphemia and her siblings would escape from doing chores at home only to go as the children of the man who

Chapter 4

gave them "the Promised Land" to watch the performing band. The children enjoyed listening and watching the actions of the band's performance while eating biscuits and drinking soda.

Euphemia loved Jehova Wanyonyi had daughters who had a natural talent for braiding hair. They would come to Euphemia's home to braid her and her sister's hair in exchange for food and milk. The sisters soon became their friends, they spent much time together.

The so acclaimed Israelites lived on Euphemia's land for years peacefully. Neither they nor Euphemia's family had any bad feelings against the other. They resided on the same land minding their own business. And by the time Euphemia was leaving home to attend college, Jehova Wanyonyi and his Lost Israelites were still residing on their land.

***

No! It wasn't easy for Euphemia to be accepted and attend college. It should have been a smooth transition, but it wasn't. It took years of hard work for her mother to make it possible, matched with perseverance and dedication from Euphemia to achieve her academic goals to accomplish the dream they both aspired for.

Euphemia had completed high school and her achievements in which, led to her acceptance into nursing school. One day out of the blue, Barasa tells Almasi and Euphemia that he would drop them off as I went to college. According to him, he was 'helping' Almasi, even though she had been ungrateful.

Euphemia remembered how happy her mother was when she heard about his intent to be present. All Euphemia could feel was sympathy for her mother as she would easily forgive her husband and jump at the chance to be embraced by him–even if it was toxic. Euphemia had a perceived notion that her father would never change.

Early the next morning, Barasa came by their house to pick up Almasi and Euphemia. The excitement left Almasi's eyes when she saw that Barasa's fifth wife was sitting in the passenger seat. Euphemia saw her mother's heart break and sighed. I knew this would happen, she thought, shaking her head. Father never fails to disappoint, she thought.

Nonetheless, Euphemia and her mother quietly sat down in the car. The whole ride, they listened to Barasa happily talking to his 'wife.' He behaved as if Almasi and Euphemia were not even there.

"How are you going to pay for Euphemia's school fees?" Barasa inquired from Almasi.

"Huh?" Almasi uttered, puzzled. "I…I thought you were going to pay for school fees?"

"What?" he shouted, looking at Almasi as if she had grown two heads. "Are you insane? Why would I pay for her school fees?"

Almasi and Euphemia were shocked at his statement. They had assumed he was going to admit Euphe-

Chapter 4

mia into the college. Euphemia was hurt that her father didn't want to provide for her college fees. He was unwilling to 'waste' money on her.

"What? Do you think I have extra money?" Barasa mocked them, staring at them from the windscreen. "I don't have any money to WASTE on you or your children."

"I cannot believe they are asking you for money," Euphemia's stepmother mocked.

"I know, sweetheart. I never knew she was so ignorant."

"Oh, my! Looks like it was a trap!"

Barasa and her stepmother both began laughing at Almasi. Their indifferent behavior wounded Euphemia. How could they do this! Mum doesn't deserve this disrespect! She turned around to look at her mother, only to get heartbroken when she saw Almasi crying silently. Slowly, Euphemia grabbed her mother's trembling hands and clutched them tightly in her hand. She squeezed it in reassurance.

"It's okay, Mum," Euphemia mouthed to her. "We will figure something out."

"Can you please drive me to the bank?" Almasi asked Barasa after calming down. Barasa, begrudgingly obliged her request. She asked Barasa to take her to a certain bank that was nearby. Almasi did not have an account in that town's bank, but she remembered working with one of the managers at a different location that had been transferred to the nearby location she was asking to be taken to.

Talk of "All things work together for those who love the lord." Euphemia did not understand what was going on. What is Mum doing? She thought, watching Almasi going toward the bank. "Walking by faith!" Half an hour later, she was surprised when her mother returned with money in her bag.

"Mum, what is this…?" Euphemia asked her.

"Don't fret, love. We are going to shop for your uniform and pay the school fees now." Her mother told her.

It wasn't just this incident that disheartened Euphemia and her mother, but the difference in the way Barasa treated his other wives and children from the way he treated Almasi and her children. Before dropping Euphemia off at school, her father decided to take them all for lunch in a very expensive restaurant. Didn't he say he does not have money? And now he is taking us to an expensive restaurant? She thought, furious. Hypocrite!

Euphemia and her mother declined to eat. They both just sat there and watched Barasa and his other wife eat silently. After they were done, Barasa dropped Euphemia back off at college. Euphemia kept thinking it was late and what would happen if her father did not take her mother home? She feared her father and her step-mother

Chapter 4

would leave her to get public transportation. Being that it was late, public transportation would be a bad option for Almasi.

However, if they left her somewhere, Almasi had no choice but to find her way home. Euphemia went to her dorm room and started praying her mom would get home safely because she knew in Kenya, robberies happened late at night. Euphemia and Almasi did not have cell phones, so there was no way of communicating and finding out whether her mother got home or not.

Petrified, Euphemia started her college life. She hoped that her mother was safe as she waited to hear from her. She knew she had no choice but to think positively and continue to work hard. It wasn't easy trying to focus knowing that her mom may not be safe; but she had to try.

Whenever Euphemia went to bed, she cried, thinking about her mother and how she was faring. Unfortunately, it was her first day in college, most adults would be excited about that, but for her, it was dreadful. All she could think about was the treatment her mother just endured and how her life would be without her.

When the school closed, Euphemia went home, and her mother told her what had happened on that day. Her fears were confirmed, Barasa went to the nearest bus station and left her mother there to use public transportation. It was frightening for Almasi; she was alone in the night by the roadside as she waited. But through God's Grace and Mercy Almasi managed to get the last bus.

She had to travel to two other public transport stations before she got home. It was late at night and she was tired and hungry when she reached home. But what worried her the most was how her daughter was handling everything. Almasi knew that Euphemia would probably be worried too and psychologically affected.

Almasi had an interesting way of dealing with negative, frustrating, and painful events; she laughed and prayed a lot to get through it. Sometimes her children would ask why she was laughing—especially with everything was going through. However, she would tell them it was the only way she could remain sane from all the things that continued to happen in her life .

Chapter 4

Chapter 5 – The Stolen Troubled Oil

"Don't let the incidents which take place in life bring you down. And certainly, don't whine. You can be brought low, that's OK, but don't be reduced by them. Just say, 'That's life.'"
~ Maya Angelou

There are certain life experiences which make things rather complex, and they have the ability to alter how individuals connect with themselves and their surroundings. These unexpected events mark life-altering instances which can change people's lives for better or worse. During such critical times, how people manage to overcome their issues is what truly matters. Over the course of time, Euphemia managed to do just that. Before going to college, a particular incident revealed she had no one to care for her except God, her mother, and siblings.

One night, Euphemia was thinking about when

Chapter 5

she had graduated from high school, she was remembering being at home with her mother and the house workers, while her siblings were away at boarding school. It was pitch dark in the night, and it proved to be rather difficult for everyone.

Euphemia could not have thought that her life would turn upside down within seconds. It was so sudden and immediate that she could not comprehend what was happening. It was around nine o'clock at night, Euphemia was having dinner with her mother in the kitchen when something unexpected happened. The house worker came running when they heard men shouting out loud at night. The only thought that came to their mind was that thugs were coming to rob them.

In an instance, strange voices echoed outside her house. Lo and behold! The police and the criminal investigating officers were in their compound. What is going on? Why are the police outside our house? she thought. She looked at her mother, but Almasi only shook her head, letting her know she also had no clue.

Not a second later, Euphemia and Almasi froze in their chairs, hearing the sound of footsteps. The footsteps were drawing closer and closer toward the front door. Why are they coming here? Did something happen? Euphemia thought.

The mother-daughter duo held their breath because they knew a storm was coming. They optimistically prayed silently, fearing for the worst. Her instinct alerted Euphemia that something wasn't right, and the complexity of the entire situation compelled her to worry even more.

Knock! Knock!

The loud knock on the front door startled them, making her and Almasi jump to their feet. Terrified, they looked at each other as fear flooded their eyes. Almasi could tell that her daughter was scared. She told Euphemia to stand behind her as she approached the front door.

"Hello, officer," Almasi greeted the brown-eyed officer as she peeked through the slightly open door. "H-how can I help you?"

"Let us inside, woman! We need to search your house for the oil!" the officer exclaimed as he growled. "Wh-what—" stuttered Almasi.

The officer, accompanied by his battalion, pushed her back with a loud bang and barged into the house. Their behavior frightened Euphemia, making her tightly clutch her mother's right arm. Our herds man Ekai and our House worker Achi came running into the living room. The number of police officers worried them.

There were about two police Land Rovers parked outside, and there were about sixteen police officers carrying wooden batons, guns, and flashlights. Gradually, they started occupying the hallway and the compound, the outside storage, and the kitchen. The once peaceful night had now become tense and deafening—there was a

Chapter 5

lot of commotion.

The brown-eyed officer glared venomously at Euphemia and her mother. All the other officers were busy ransacking the house, and they were eyeballing everything. They stood before Almasi and Euphemia with their guns, and it was quite evident they were awaiting orders to apprehend.

"Where is the refugee cooking oil?" a brown-eyed officer asked us. They had their guns raised and they were prepared for anything at that moment.

"W-we don't know!" Almasi replied while clutching her daughter's hand and pushing her behind.

"We d-don't know what you are t-talking about," Almasi added.

"DON'T LIE!" the officer exclaimed. "We have information that a trailer truck carrying refugee oil came to your home."

Euphemia and her mother were shaken to the core. They could hardly utter a word. It was their first time interacting with law enforcement officers. Suddenly, Almasi started hyperventilating, shaking her head left to right, and Euphemia pursued similar actions. They were attempting to tell the officers that they didn't know anything.

The brown-eyed officer turned toward the other officers and shouted, "SEARCH THE HOUSE!"

The other officers acknowledged the orders and started moving throughout the house. Four of them began talking while others moved from one room to another. Euphemia didn't know what was going on. She would glance from one person to the other perplexed by what was going on. She thought about calling her father for a second, but she dismissed the thought—she knew that her father would never help them.

"M-mum?" Euphemia stutteringly called out to her mother.

"Yes, darling?" Almasi answered while caressing her daughter's hair.

"Why are the officers here? Did we do something wrong?" Euphemia inquired.

"No, no," Almasi shook her head. "Don't worry, nothing's wrong. It will be alright."

However, the agitation on her mother's face compelled Euphemia to think otherwise.

While Almasi, Euphemia, Ekai, and Achi were hurdled in the corner of the room, the officers kicked down another door. Even though Euphemia and Almasi feared for the worst, they tried to stay focused on each other and ignored everyone else. Every one or two minutes, they would jump into a state of fright because the officers were destroying the house. Euphemia was troubled because the officers were breaking everything while they were busy searching for the 'cooking oil.'

Chapter 5

Why are they even searching for cooking oil in our house? she thought.

She sat beside her mother, and she started praying that the police officers wouldn't kill them; they were scared to death. After fifteen minutes, they heard the officers coming back to the living room. They walked toward the brown-eyed officer while towing loads of cooking oils.

"What!" Euphemia thought as her eyes widened with horror.

"Where did they come from? I did not know we had this much," her train of thoughts ceased as she gazed at her mother's face.

Almasi was profusely sweating as guilt and remorse became quite apparent in her eyes.

"We found the Cooking Oil!" one of them told the blue-eyed officer. "It was hidden in the large storage room."

The blue-eyed officer nodded at them, and he ordered an immediate arrest of Almasi.

An officer stepped forward, keeping his fingers firmly on the revolver's trigger, and he shouted, "You are under arrest for stealing cooking oil from the port that was being delivered to a refugee camp!"

"Wh-what!" Almasi stuttered. "But this isn't my

house! M-my husband was the one who brought the goods. We had no idea it was cooking oil!"

"We don't want any excuses," the officer retorted.

"I am not giving any excuses! Please, officer, hear me out!" Almasi looked at the brown-eyed officer. "That oil belongs to my husband. You can ask him; he was the one who ordered the transport oil…."

"Stop lying!"

"We have already asked the man who you are implying to be your husband, and he told us that he did not authorize any transportation or storage and that this house belongs to you. He has no connection with anything in your house."

"Wh-what? H-he cannot d-do this," Almasi shook her head in disbelief.

Almasi was struck by disbelief because Barasa had done something so heinous. If only she had known that Barasa would masquerade as an innocent man and had a clue that it was a crafty deal to store the cooking oil at the house in which she lived, she wouldn't have allowed him. The officer handcuffed Almasi, making Euphemia cry in despair.

"Mum!" she cried, as she ran after her mother and grabbed her arms. "No, please don't take her. MOTHER!" Euphemia added further.

Chapter 5

The officers didn't listen to the teenager and forcefully pushed her aside. "Mum!" Euphemia shouted as she stood up from the floor and started running toward Almasi. "Please," Euphemia begged for her mother's immediate release.

Achi grabbed Euphemia and embraced her into her arms. She held back the sobbing teen from going after the officers as she knew that Euphemia would face the consequences if she offended them. Euphemia kept stretching her hands toward her mother. The entire sight of her mother being dragged out of the house was nothing but pure agony.

"Mum, no. No, mum!" Euphemia kept on mumbling.

"Please, no, mum, please…." Euphemia cried in Achi's arms because everything was too much for her to handle.

After a few minutes of trying to comprehend what had just happened, Euphemia and Achi remembered some oil was still hidden in the outside store. They feared that if the police came back, there would be worse consequences. Achi suggested they carry the oil and dispose of it in the garden.

Euphemia, Achi, and Ekai gathered courage in the pitch darkness and started taking the oil out and pouring it out on the farm. While they were almost three-quarters, they heard a sigh as if someone was approaching. They all thought they had been caught; they became frightened and sat directly on the dirty floor, trembling. After a few minutes, Ekai gathered courage and decided to go out and check, only to realize it was just the cows breathing and sighing. They all sighed in relief and continued to pour out the oil until it was all gone.

They still could not comprehend what had just happened a few hours ago. Euphemia prayed that it was all a dream and her mother was okay. Euphemia took a little nap because she was overwhelmed and sleeping seemed like the right choice. When she woke up, she went into the living room.

Reality sunk in"Euph?" Achi called her.

"MUM!" Euphemia trailed off. "Mum isn't here, is she?" Euphemia added, Achi shook her head no. There was sympathy and anguish in her eyes, but she feared for Euphemia. "I am sorry, Euph," said Achi with a thick rasp of sadness in her voice.

"Wh-what happened when I slept?" she asked, glancing around the room. "Where is Ekai?"

"Ekai left. He went to his house," Achi told her. "Your father came after your mother…."

"What! Why?" Euphemia suddenly was overjoyed, thinking that her father was there to save her mother.

"Where is he now? Did he go to the police station? Is he going to bail my mother out?" Euphemia

Chapter 5

tossed a series of questions.

Then Achi quietly gazed at the innocent teen, who was foolishly delighted because she thought her father would help them. "Oh, Euph!" Achi thought. "If only you knew!"

"No, your father…your father didn't come for your mother." Achi gulped when she saw the perplexity on Euphemia's face. She knew it would be hard to tell her the truth, but it was her right—she needed to know. "Mr. Barasa came and took the oil he hid. He…." Achi continued talking. However, Euphemia couldn't hear anything else. Her mind was stuck on the fact that her father cared about the cooking oil rather than her mother. It was at that time a deep hatred began to stir in her heart. She knew her father didn't love them, but she thought he cared about them.

How foolish I was! Euphemia thought.

"Euph?" said Achi with no response from her. She continued to be lost in her own thoughts. "Euph?" She shook her gently and said, "Euphemia!"

Euphemia snapped out of her daydream trance, realizing Achi was calling for her. She looked at Achi's tired eyes and responded, "Yes?"

"I-I have to go, sweetheart," Achi told her apologetically. "I-I am sorry, but…but I cannot stay the night."

Euphemia paused because she knew Achi had to

go back to her home to her children.

"All right," she mumbled. "You can go."
"I am sorry. I will pray Mrs. Almasi gets bailed," Achieng added further.

Euphemia watched Achi leave sluggishly, it was breaking her heart to leave her alone. Her eyes strolled around the large, dark and empty house. Petrified, she ran toward her room and slid down under the bed. Euphemia pulled herself into a fetal position. One after the other, tears kept streaming from her eyes. She lied down in her bed alone under the bed in the dark of night!

While under the bed, Euphemia heard her father's car, the Range Rover coming at high speed, he knew where Euphemia's bedroom was. He came with lights, glared at her bedroom window, and then called out her name. Euphemia was excited her father had come back to stay with her.
However, it was not the case.

Barasa shouted from the car for Euphemia to open the window; when she did, he just told her it would be okay, only for Euphemia to realize he had come back to try and take the remaining oil. He went to the outside store, took the oil, and while doing so, he heard something in the bushes and thought the police had returned or were waiting around.

Scared, Barasa immediately covered his number plate with a blanket and took a shortcut with a narrow makeshift bridge that usually allowed smaller vehicles.

Chapter 5

She was perplexed at how he made it through, only God knows. Euphemia heard of this getaway from Achi and the neighbors the following day since it was a small village; everyone had learned of the commotion.

Why? Euphemia asked herself while she sobbed excessively that night.

Mum had never wronged anyone. She never thought bad about anyone. Then why? What did father gain with this? What was he trying to prove? Does he not wish well for us at all? thought Euphemia as she went through the state of her prevalent impediment.

The police had arrested Almasi because Barasa alluded to polygamy and stated t it was Almasi's home; he denied any kind of involvement. Yet it was realized that Barasa had colluded with a young man, a neighbor that was more or less a gangster. The two were working with other well-known people in the lucrative oil businesses from a nearby town to derail and hijack the oil truck and sell the oil on the black markets.

For Euphemia, it was not surprising because of how her father had treated them in the past, but it still hurt her—knowing t he never cared about her mother, her, or her siblings. What shocked her the most was he went to jeopardize her mother as well as her siblings. It made her realize the degree of hate and disregard that Barasa had for her family.

It was a difficult night for Euphemia, and she wept until she became tired and fell asleep.

***

Euphemia was just eighteen years old; she was still a child. The dreadful thing for her was the stream of questions that she had to face from her siblings. They were supposed to arrive that day, and it worried her about how she would handle them. Every time they came back from boarding school, they would look for their mother. Euphemia was immediately alerted when she felt the creaking of the door.

Oh, no! Euphemia thought. They are here!

"Mom!" Zion shouted as he ran into the house.

"Slow down, will you?" Baraka yelled while shaking his head. "You are going to hurt yourself," he added.

"I want to see mom," Ivy demanded in a manner that was quite exciting. "I have something to tell her!"

"No! I will tell her first," Ezra grumbled. "You told her first last time. Now, it's my turn," he added.

"No!" "Mom!" "Please!" The children kept screaming, and this was causing a headache for Euphemia. She was getting paranoid with each passing second. Baraka noticed something; he turned toward his elder sister and shook her.

"Sis?" he called Euphemia.

"Where is mom?" asked Baraka.

Chapter 5

Suddenly, the remaining siblings unconsciously alerted themselves upon hearing Baraka's inquiry. They turned toward her with eagerness. Euphemia could see the curiousness behind their eyes, and she could tell that they longed for their mother.

"S-she-e…," Euphemia paused. "M-mom…she, she…is not here."

"What? Then where is she," Baraka asked.

Euphemia took a deep breath, and she started telling her siblings about what had happened. She watched several emotions fade in and out through their facial expressions and finally stopped because it was too painful for her to explain what had happened. She knew it was going to be a long week ahead. The younger siblings were annoyed and helpless; they were inconsolable. Euphemia and Baraka tried their best to keep them calm.

***

Euphemia remembered she had an aunt who was called Maisha—her father's sister—who lived in a different city. She decided to go and see her and ask for help. Maisha was well off, and she lived in the luxurious part of the city. Sometimes her family would visit them over the weekend to stay. When they would go to visit, their aunt always cooked food for them.

Euphemia knew her, and she realized her aunt was her last hope of saving her mother. If her father wasn't willing to get her mother out, then Euphemia had to step forward. She had to fight for her mother.

The following day, Euphemia took public transportation and went to see her aunt. Her aunt greeted her as soon as she opened the door for her. She took her niece inside and into the kitchen. Maisha instructed Euphemia to relax back at the kitchen table while she cooked something for her.

"Aunt," Euphemia called her. "I...I have a favor to ask."

"Yes, darling, what is it?" Maisha smiled at her niece. "You can ask me anything."
"Aunt," Euphemia trailed off and caught her aunt's attention. "Can you, please, let me know the whereabouts of my mom, and if...if not, then can you help me?"

"Euphemia," Maisha sighed. "You don't need to worry about that, dear."

"B-but—"

"Just go home, Euph. Your mom...your dad is going to bring your mom back home. He is going to bail her soon," said Euphemia's aunt.

I don't know, Euphemia thought. "I highly doubt that father will even bother to bail her out of jail." While Euphemia was leaving her Aunt told her that her step mothers will stop by to check on them.

Euphemia's two stepmothers later the following day arrived to bring her and her siblings food. They would turn up to see how the children were doing and

Chapter 5

then leave shortly after. For almost an entire week, Euphemia and her siblings were home alone.

Under pressure from family and friends, Barasa decided to go out of his way to bail Almasi from jail. Euphemia had no idea how that played out, but her mother came home the following day. And the day after was when Euphemia was scheduled to go to college. From the previous chapter you can remember what happened the day Euphemia went to College.

Chapter 6 – Mistakes

"Loss eventually arrives when something departs. Grief is working through both. To die is as if one's eyes had been put out, and one cannot see anything anymore. Perhaps it is like being shut in a cellar. One is abandoned by all. They have slammed the door and are gone. One does not see anything and notices only the damp smell of putrefaction."
~ Edvard Munch

Mistakes. We all make them, right?
Making and learning from mistakes is necessary for the human experience. We can take lessons from our failures and wrong decisions can teach us the most valuable life lessons. Mistakes do occur unexpectedly and without our knowledge. The only method to prevent making them is to stop living but that is also a mistake.

And that was what Euphemia learned when she made a decision that almost ruined her life.

Chapter 6

***

On the first day of college when Euphemia arrived, she was grouped with the people who got there first. It was a sunny day, and the sky was clear, and the wind blew softly in a steady rhythm. The sun was shining radiantly, spreading its warmth everywhere. She gazed at her surroundings as the students lingered around the campus, talking and laughing with their peers.

Euphemia sighed; "Hello!" She heard a voice and turned around curiously. A boy in his teens was walking toward her. He had a beautiful smile on his face.

"Hey!" Euphemia greeted him back.

"My name is Ashura. I haven't seen you here in this town. Are you new?"

"I am Euphemia." She shook his outstretched hand. "Uh, yes, you're right. I am new here."

"Hmm, I see you are lost," he hummed. "Don't worry; I can show you around if you want."

He was friendly and nice, Euphemia thought. There is something about him that brings peace. I couldn't pinpoint it, but he seemed like a long-lost brother.

"Alright!" she replied and went along with him. Euphemia had heard someone saying, 'When you are new in college, the first person you meet will be your best friend.' She never believed in that myth; she thought it was bizarre. However, over the years, she realized it was true. The first person she met—Ashura—became her best friend. He found her alone and lost in a new place and welcomed her with open arms.

Ashura was such a polite person. Being around him made Euphemia confident; he would encourage and support her—especially when she felt low. He would always warn her from having bad friends, including those interested in only having love relationships with her. Ashura became her mentor and protected her like a brother.

***

One day, as Euphemia was going to the dorm, she heard a familiar voice calling her name.

"Euphemia?"

Who? She thought. Why does it seem so familiar? She turned and was shocked to find her ex-boyfriend standing in front of her.

"S-sarki?" she stammered, dumfounded. "What are you doing here?"

"I-I was here to meet a relative," he uttered, beaming at her. "I didn't know I would be fortunate enough to meet you."

Euphemia's heart skipped a beat, but she forced herself to suppress her emotions. *No, Euphemia, you cannot let him have the upper hand. You broke up with him,*

Chapter 6

remember? You need to focus on your studies.

"Well...," Sarki began saying after a long awkward silence. "What are you doing here? Did you people shift?"
"No, no." She shook her head. "We didn't. I'm actually going to college over here." She swallowed nervously.

"Oh, okay." Sarki gave her a faint smile. "I hope we can meet each other again."

"Yeah, I do too," she replied.

After that, the two parted ways. But it ignited a spark in Euphemia's heart again. Entering her door room, she laid down on the bed and began recalling when she first met him.

***

It was a year ago, when Euphemia was still in high school and she saw Sarki for the first time. It was a faint crush she had developed for him that later turned into love.

Her mother, Almasi, was a corn farmer and would hire trucks to take it to the market once she had shelled them. Almasi would then call the truck owner to pick up the corn and deliver it to the market. Euphemia watched her mother work so hard year after year selling her crop to the market.

One day as Euphemia watched the trucks load the corn while sitting on the verandah. Euphemia saw a young teen guy climbing out of the owner's truck. They both strolled toward Almasi.

Who is that? Euphemia thought. As if the guy had heard her thoughts, he glanced in her direction. Oh, shoot! She instantly lowered her head, blushing in embarrassment. What the heck? Have I been caught red-handed? Shoot! I hope he hasn't seen me. After a few minutes went by, she peeked at him and was surprised to find a hint of a smirk on his face. She gulped; he wasn't looking at her, but the cheeky smile told her what she feared the most.

Euphemia let out a sigh in relief when she saw them leaving. She thought she was done with it and she won't have to see him again. However, she didn't know it was only the start of a new relationship.

After that day, she would often see the guy coming to the field. Initially, she ignored him and continued looking out for her mother. Nevertheless, she couldn't avoid his prying eyes on her. It would make her conscious but, on the other hand, also excited her. What was this feeling? She couldn't understand why she was getting attached to him. What was it about him that was making him look so attractive? She couldn't have known that yet. Euphemia didn't know how and when, but she was unintentionally falling for him.

When it got evident their feelings were somehow mutual for one another, the owner's son decided to make a move. One Sunday morning, when Almasi and the truck owner were busy unloading the corn—5 kms away—Euphemia saw her 'crush' approaching her.

Chapter 6

Oh my God! She thought, and with widened eyes, she gaped at him. He is coming over here! What... what am I going to do? Think Euphemia, think. She was getting unnerved and anxious. Okay, alright, calm down. She took a deep breath and gave herself a pep talk. You can do it, girl. It's just a guy, not a bull or a dog; he won't kill you. Relax and keep your head up high.

"Hey!" The guy greeted her, smiling widely.

"H-hi!" Euphemia replied, stammering. What the heck? She wanted to facepalm herself. Didn't I just give myself a pep talk a minute ago?

"I am Sarki." He grinned. "As you must have already known, I am the owner's son."

"Oh, yes," she uttered, staring at him.
A second passed, and Sarki raised an eyebrow in question. It was then that Euphemia realized she was supposed to introduce herself. Oh, Euph, what am I going to do with you!

"I-I am Euphemia," she murmured. "I am Almasi's daughter."

"Euphemia? What a beautiful name!"

"Thank you!" She blushed at the compliment and smiled.

"So...."

They both continued their conversation until Sarki had to depart. However, Euphemia and Sarki promised to stay in touch and meet again. It was the start of a love that bloomed inside them and formed a relationship. They became close over that year, and their passion got more vital day by day.

Unfortunately, a lack of miscommunication broke them apart. When Euphemia went to college, they stopped talking to each other for almost two years. She would still think about him when she was a freshman in college. But as she got busier, she slowly began to forget about him.

***

I still cannot believe it, Euphemia thought, sighing, sitting up on her bed. He is here; I saw him again. She smiled faintly. What if he is here for me? What if he was also missing me and wanted to be with me? She squealed and jumped up from the bed. Does he still love me?

Euphemia was lost in her daydream, thinking about what-ifs, not knowing what the future held for her, possible…for them. She believed Sarki still loved and cared for her. She was unaware of what thunderous storm was marching up in her direction.

A week later, Euphemia met Sarki again; this time, it was at a café. She was drinking her hot chocolate and reading a book when she noticed a person's silhouette. Startled, she glanced up and was surprised to find a grinning Sarki standing in front of her table.

Chapter 6

"H-hey!" she uttered. I guess some things never change.

"Hi!" he replied enthusiastically. He looked at the empty seat and said, "If you don't mind, can I accompany you?"

"Um, sure. I don't mind." She beamed.

Months passed, and they began to see each other again. It was the same thing all over again. Euphemia was head over heels for him. She was unable to stop the feelings and emotions from coming back. She never knew that soon she would regret her decision, acknowledging it was an awful mistake.

Sarki was living in another town miles away from where Euphemia resided. On the day the couple was out on a date, they kept discussing how difficult it was for them to date. When out of nowhere, Sarki proposed an unusual scheme.

"I have an idea for you," he commented, gazing at her.

"Huh?" she muttered quizzically. "An idea?"

"Yes, something that will benefit both of us!"

"Alright, what is it?"

"How about switching colleges, and going to the college that is next to my home."

"What?" Euphemia exclaimed, flabbergasted. "Are you out of your mind? What are you talking about?"

"I know, I know, calm down, babe." Sarki took her face in his hands and propelled her to look at him. "I can understand that you think the idea is absurd but think about this." He paused and took a deep breath and continued to say, "Right now, we both can hardly make time for one another. If you go to the same college but next to my home, we'll be able to spend more time with each other. It'll be beneficial for us, babe."

It was startling for her; she doubted if the idea was safe. Euphemia paused, thinking about Sarki's proposal thoroughly. He isn't wrong about this, she thought. We are usually so busy that we cannot even talk for more than an hour. If we can hang out as much as we want with this, then what is the harm?

"Alright!" She agreed, smiling at him. "I'll come with you!"

Her instincts told her otherwise. A dreadful feeling entered her stomach, telling her the decision could be wrong. However, Euphemia was in love; she dismissed her gut feelings, thinking it was just the 'jitteriness' talking.

Oh, if only she had known what was stored ahead, she would've never taken such a drastic step! Within a week, Euphemia ended up following him to his town. She was excited to meet his family and begin a life with him. She dropped out of college hoping to get accepted to

Chapter 6

a college next to his home where she and her boyfriend would visit each other often, especially over the weekend.

Who knew this would be the start of a destructive life for Euphemia's career path?

***

The next few weeks were blissful for Euphemia; she enjoyed spending time with Sarki in his town. They would go on dates and spend time with her parents and sister. Things were going well until something strange happened.

After attempting in vain to get Euphemia acceptance into the new college, Euphemia's plan was to then go back to her previous college. It was the day when Euphemia and Sarki were supposed to leave for college. She was scared of the thought of going back to her previous college and if she would get accepted back; however, dread filled her when she looked for Sarki. They had promised to go together to the college, but he wasn't around.

Where is he? She thought, looking around. Did he go ahead without me? Euphemia searched for him all over the house, but she couldn't find him. W-w-where is Sarki? Why is he not here? Tears began flowing from her eyes. Did something happen? Betrayal?

As if a light bulb had switched on, she ran to find Sarki's mother. And the moment she saw her, she asked about Sarki's whereabouts. Euphemia was startled as soon as she heard what Sarki's mother had to say. "Sarki?" His mother, Abuya, asked, confused. "I saw him leave early in the morning. Didn't he tell you?"

"Wh-here did he g-go?" Euphemia asked.

"I don't know, sweetheart. He said he has to run an urgent errand."

Euphemia couldn't believe what she was hearing. How could he do this to her? He told her he would be there for her; so why?

When the day came for Euphemia to go back to college, Sarki had disappeared. The errand he went away for he was gone for two weeks. Euphemia was shaken; she didn't know what to do. She had no money to go back to college; it was miles away. What terrified her the most was the fact that her mother Almasi had no idea Euphemia had dropped out of school. Especially what she had gone through to admit her into college.

What would her mother think or do if she came to know what her daughter had done? Or worse, when she would get to know that Euphemia had dropped out of college? It was then Euphemia realized she had dug her own grave.

***

There was nothing else to do she had to resolve her problem to do the scariest thing she had ever done in her life. Go back Home! One day, when Sarki's parents were going to the market, Euphemia asked them a favor.

Chapter 6

"I don't want to be a burden to you both anymore," she told them.

"Can you please take me to Afaafa's house?"

Abuya and Feye Sarki's parents were kind and humble; they could feel that Euphemia was scared. They agreed and dropped her off at Afaafa's— Sarki's sister— she lived in a nearby town that was closer to Euphemia's home. Euphemia couldn't help but be thankful to them even though their son had abandoned her.

When Euphemia got to the town, she met Afaafa and stayed over for one week until Sarki reappeared. She was furious when she saw him; she asked him again and again why he left. However, his only reply was, "I am sorry, I had no choice." But would a mere 'sorry' bring back the emptiness she felt? Would it ever mend her broken heart that was ripped into tiny pieces? No, it won't. Euphemia was more than aware of it.

She was so disappointed she was unwilling to open her heart to him again. Euphemia wanted to go home, but she was afraid as she had been away for almost a month now. It meant she must have been suspended from college.

After what seemed like days, Euphemia finally got the courage. She gathered her things and decided to go home. Let's face it, she thought. No matter what, it was my mistake, and I needed to accept it. I have to endure it and it is now or never.

***

A few days later, Euphemia gathered the courage and went home with all her belongings. She was so scared, thinking her mother was going to swallow her alive. She dreaded her mother would question the things she had no answer for.

Lord, please help me! Euphemia thought and knocked on the door. Not a minute later, the door opened, and Almasi greeted her daughter. Instinctively, Euphemia closed her eyes, dreading the worst. However, she was shocked that Almasi embraced her.

"My baby!" Almasi cried, tightening the hold on her daughter but not enough to suffocate her.

Euphemia sniffed and let out a sob; she wrapped her arms around her mother—pouring out all her pain. The mother-daughter duo cried for hours. After they had calmed down, Almasi brought her daughter inside.

"Sit, Euph," Almasi told her. "I will bring you something to eat."

Euphemia saw her mother disappearing into the kitchen. She was both relieved and tensed to reveal the truth. She waited until her mother returned, contemplating how to tell her everything.

"Mom, I—"

"No, no," Almasi interrupted her, shaking her head. "I don't want to listen to anything. I am so happy

Chapter 6

to see you, my baby! I don't care about anything, alright? Just relax and leave everything to me. Your mother is going to take care of everything."

Euphemia sighed, understanding that it wasn't the right time. She observed how pleased her mother was to see her. She did not say anything until after one week when she told Almasi about what had happened. They were in the garden, gazing at the colorful flowers, when she gathered the courage and decided to tell her mother. "Mum…," Euphemia mumbled, lowering her head in shame. "I have to tell you something." A pause. "I-I messed up."

"Yes, darling," Almasi cooed, patting her daughter's hand in reassurance. "You can tell your mother anything. Your mother is always going to have your back, no matter what you do."

"Mum, I-I…,"

Euphemia began telling her mother everything, from the start of her college days, to when she met Sarki and how she went to his town.

"Oh, my!" Almasi exclaimed, covering her mouth with her hand. "Euphemia, you…." She paused, lost for words. But when she saw her daughter's torn expressions, she redeemed herself and uttered, "Alright, alright. It's okay; you are okay. That's all that matters right now. At least you can go back to the college—"

"Mum," Euphemia said in a monotone voice. "I

am not going back to college."

"What?"

"I…I dropped out."

Almasi paled, almost fainting, but she became conscious of her surroundings before she could. For the next few weeks that followed, there was much tension and lack of words for both mother and daughter. Euphemia had no idea what her mother was thinking and what she was planning for her.

Her mother being the adult and parent had to figure out how to help her daughter. She started by informing her daughter they had to find a way for her to get back into the same college. At this point Euphemia had lost hope and given up on returning to college. Almasi encouraged her daughter—despite what she did—but Euphemia was doubtful she could get accepted back. She sometimes regretfully became so mean and spiteful to her mother whenever the topic was brought up. Nonetheless, Almasi was a mother; she couldn't leave her daughter like that.

When things started to calm down, Almasi took Euphemia back to college and begged the head teacher in college to take her back. Then after much persuasion and promises, they took Euphemia back. Fortunately, she hadn't missed much of the coursework as she had just started her junior year.

However, what she lost was beyond that!

Chapter 6

Her pride and self-esteem!

Chapter 7– What's Love

"Ask me to define my love for you, and I'll say it's captured in every beautiful memory of our past, detailed out in vivid visions of our dreams and future plans, but most of all, it's right now, at the moment where everything I've ever wanted in my life is standing right in front of me."
~ Leo Christopher

When people care, trust and feel compassion for other individuals, it is defined as 'Love.' Each living being, animal or human, needs a bit of attention and affection. Love is also omnipotent and omniscient; it can be found in many different forms. It doesn't matter how strong a person is on the outside; they need someone to love. A soul that lacks love is like a vase without flowers. Love perhaps holds the most significant value in our life.

Similarly, Euphemia—who was heartbroken and devastated before—found comfort in a new love. She

Chapter 7

wouldn't have imagined after having been betrayed before, she could ever find someone who truly loves her. However, by the time she turned twenty-two, she met Thabiti—her true love.

***

After returning to college, Euphemia busied herself with school work. She regretted her actions of dropping out of college and what had happened in the previous month. However, she didn't lose hope and she studied hard for her upcoming exams.

Her best friend, Ashura, was there to help and support her. After she told him the reason for her disappearance, Ashura went into a protective role. From that day, he didn't let Sarki or anyone come close to her. He ensured that Euphemia did not get any distractions which would make her derail from college. Euphemia was more than happy to have a friend like him in her life.

Days turned into months, and months turned into the next year; Euphemia made it to her third year in college. She had slowly but painfully forgotten about her traumatizing past relationship. During these last years, she learned self-worth and understood what self-love was. She promised herself she would not fall in love anytime with anyone soon. And even if she did, the significant half would have to prove himself first! Euphemia wasn't willing to allow anyone into her heart anymore.

One day, when she was strolling in the campus garden, she noticed someone not familiar to her walking nearby. Hmm? She thought to herself, a stranger-should

I run for my life or prepare to fight if attacked? Who is this person coming right at me? She peeked from her peripheral vision and noticed a young handsome guy in his mid-twenties gazing at her. What the…? Okay, Euph, calm down. Just pretend you haven't seen him and continue walking.

However, before she could step forward, the stranger started making his way directly toward her. Astonished, Euphemia clutched the strap of her backpack tightly. She slid the bag from her shoulder and brought it in front of her.

One….

Two….

Three—

Euphemia turned around quickly and flung the bag at the guy. As if it was a slow-mo, the stranger flew in the air and landed on the floor. A large gash was visible on his face. If it were any other day or occasion, Euphemia would've laughed, however, today for some reason it wasn't the day.

"W-who are you?" she stammered, observing the unfamiliar person. "What d-do you want?"

The guy gripped his bruised cheek and glanced up. Euphemia had thought he would threaten her or, worse, beat her, but that wasn't the case. There was no hate or disdain in his body language, aside from the glint

Chapter 7

of 'amusement' that passed through his eyes swiftly. "I am Thabiti," the guy answered, smiling faintly.

Alright, and? she thought, uncertain as to why he was telling her that.

"I don't think you have seen me before." A pause. "I am here accompanying my colleague who is visiting his girlfriend."

Shoot! Euphemia's skin got pale. Oh my God! What have I done? visiting? Really Euphemia? She glanced around her, relieved that no one had seen them. She feared that if someone got to learn about what had happened, she would be bullied. There was already a rumor in the college that some men who worked nearby at a bank would visit the college looking for young women to date. She had tried to steer clear from men for years, but now she landed herself into trouble with this young very sweet gentleman.

"Hey?" Thabiti called her, waving his hand to pull her out of the daydream. "Are you still here?"

"I-I…," Euphemia started saying, swallowing. "I am s-sorry!" She lowered her head and closed her eyes. "I…I didn't know who you were, please, forgive me. I was—"

A melodic laugh interrupted her, and she opened her eyes. Thabiti was chuckling and gazing at her with what seemed to be 'adoration.' Huh? Euphemia thought. Why is he laughing? Oh no, don't tell me! Did the smack affect his brain?

"I know what you're thinking right now," Thabiti murmured. "And no, I haven't gone mad." Euphemia blushed furiously. "Your hands are light, I swear; it couldn't even hurt a bee."

"Oh," she replied.

"Anyways, it's my fault. I shouldn't have acted like that." He scratched his head sheepishly. "I…I just wanted to talk to you."

"Me?" Euphemia uttered puzzled. "I don't understand. We don't even know each other."

"Actually…I know you." Thabiti smiled, and she raised an eyebrow in question. "I-I mean, I have often seen you outside campus as I walked by from work and have always wanted to talk to you."

"Uh, sure."

They walked to the parking lot, talking all the while. Euphemia was relieved to know that he wasn't a wicked person. Phew! She sighed. Thank God he isn't that bad.

The strange incident was the start of a beautiful relationship. Euphemia and Thabiti wouldn't have known that their friendship would turn into something more years later.

Chapter 7

After months when Euphemia and Thabiti had become good friends, he told her he knew her. He had known about her the moment she stepped into college. However, no matter how hard he tried over the years, he couldn't gather the courage to approach her. The more he spoke to her, the more he found her fascinating and pleasant. It was the first time Thabiti admired someone, but he was afraid she wouldn't accept his friendship. He would talk to Euphemia's classmates and get to know her from them.

The more he knew about her, the deeper he fell for her! It wasn't until the third year Thabitia compelled himself to reach out to Euphemia—as, before this, he knew she had a boyfriend. He respected her privacy and didn't want to come between them. Nevertheless, he heard from his peers that Euphemia had dropped out of school and broke up with her boyfriend.

It was then that Thabiti decided that it was now or never. He mustered up the courage to reach out to her instead. He knew she was hurt because of her past, so he befriended her before getting into a relationship with her.

***

Euphemia impatiently waited three years and two months for Thabiti to propose to her. She could feel that he also felt the same way she did. She could feel it; it was there. She was waiting for him to tell her how much he loved her.

Thabiti was a handsome and well-dressed man. He would often dress up in office wear and a well-kempt jacket. Euphemia had never seen him shout or be aggressive at anyone. He spoke in such a soft and gentle voice that everyone wanted to talk to him. The best thing she liked about him was that he listened—every time—he would take his time and be very patient.

Euphemia was fond of his contagious smile, and everyone spoke well about him. Thabiti was a kind-hearted person, so selfless and down to earth. He had never thought anyone was bad, evil, or could do wrong. Fortunately, or unfortunately, depending on your perspective, in Euphemia's perspective, he still was and will forever be the same on those lines. He gave everyone the benefit of the doubt, always went out of his way to help others, and enjoyed spending a lot of time helping others.

Euphemia and Thabiti's friends would joke around that Euphemia would marry someone secretly and wouldn't invite them. They all would tease her to tell them who was the 'one.' However, she would just blush and smile. It always made Thabiti jealous, but he would try to suppress it. He didn't want anyone to know about his feelings, but it was more prominent than he would've ever imagined.

One day, Euphemia and Thabiti and their friends went on a vacation to a different town. It was a nice getaway for them as they all had been exhausted because of the exams. Finally! Euphemia thought, gazing at the beach from the hotel balcony. I can breathe in the fresh air now!

"Hey!" Thabiti called her, coming to stand beside

Chapter 7

her.

"Oh, hey!" Euphemia voiced.

"What are you doing?" he asked, gazing at her curiously.

"Nothing much." She sighed. "Just taking in the beautiful view of the beach."

"It's beautiful, isn't it?"

"It is."

They went quiet and admired the sun slowly disappearing into the clouds.

"Are you free tomorrow?" Thabiti asked suddenly. "Huh?" Euphemia said, turning to him. "Yeah, I am. Why?"

"Um, actually, we haven't been out for a long time." He paused. "I mean…you and me, alone. If you don't mind, can we hang out tomorrow?"

"Sure!" Euphemia answered a little too eagerly. And the next day, as promised, Euphemia and Thabiti went on a day trip to an upcountry town. It was a romantic spot that Euphemia fell in love with. They spent the day strolling the old streets. It was eye-catching for them, especially for Euphemia, as she had never been out of her hometown.

When it was one o'clock, Thabiti took her to a small and simple restaurant for dinner. Euphemia was surprised he had already booked the place. They enjoyed their lunch, laughing and making new memories.
At night, they went to the beach to view the night sky and sunset. The view was awe-gazing for Euphemia; she smiled fondly, looking at them. Thabiti, who was gazing at her, smiled adoringly at her—as if she was his moon. Euphemia walked closer to the lake to graze her foot in the cold water. The tingling sensation brought peace to her mind—she was pleased and grateful.

I should get back now, Euphemia thought, fifteen minutes later. She turned and glanced at where Thabiti was sitting, writing something on the sand. Huh? What is he doing? She thought and began walking toward him. Before she could reach him, Thabiti stood up and grinned at her.

What is wrong with him? she thought.
"Come…," Thabiti whispered.

Euphemia was puzzled at first, but the more she got closer, she realized what was written on the sad. Tears began brimming in her eyes when she stared at the letters,

"Will you be my girlfriend?"

Euphemia didn't know whether to laugh or cry. She had been waiting for this day, and now it was here. Instantly, she looked him in the eye and said, 'yes.' Thabiti beamed at her and took her into his arms.

Chapter 7

"I love you, Euphemia," he mumbled.

"I love you too, Thabiti," she murmured back.

The new couple sealed their love with a kiss.

***

One year after dating, Euphemia and Thabiti moved in together. Their new life was blissful. In that one-bedroom apartment, the couple made memories—ones they would never forget. They enjoyed taking long walks together and would walk miles together. It would allow them to admire nature and spend time with each other. They would sometimes speculate and make jokes about how they have walked around the world in circles over a million times.

Euphemia and Thabiti loved walking and would walk many places in search of ice cream. They shared the same love of vanilla ice cream as their favorite flavor. However over time pistachio ice cream became one the favorite flavors added to their list to eat while walking.

Whenever Euphemia and Thabiti got bored in the house, they would wander aimlessly. If they were just sitting in the house, they would suddenly come up with a plan to climb a hill or walk the streets. From time to time, Euphemia and Thabiti would remember their fond places when they had no money but only 20 shillings. They would go and find a place to eat some French fries loaded with vinegar, condiment mixture, and red chili pepper with the money they had.

Chapter 8 – New Life

"To be pregnant is to be vitally alive, thoroughly woman, and distressingly inhabited. Soul and spirit are stretched – along with body – making pregnancy a time of transition, growth, and profound beginnings."
~ Anne Christian Buchanan

When a woman gives birth to a baby, she enters a new phase of her life. It involves all the obligations of fostering the newborn and providing adequate love and compassion. Motherhood furthermore entails providing constant directions to the child for them to conquer hardships and challenges as the child grows up.

Becoming a mother is one of God's greatest gifts, and parents are perhaps the most special people in a child's life. To be a mother entails numerous difficulties, challenges, and sacrifices. A mother is tenacious and assures security for her child to help fight and survive in the

Chapter 8

world.

It was what Euphemia experienced when a new life began growing inside her.

***

One day Euphemia went home to visit her mom. And as a mother's instinct, Almasi immediately understood something was different with her. She observed her daughter's mood shifts and the change in her routines and habits. Almasi quickly concluded that Euphemia was pregnant. It wasn't showing, but she sure was.

Once when Euphemia was lying on a bench in the courtyard, Almasi walked there and decided to talk to her daughter. She knew it couldn't be helped

"Are you pregnant?" Almasi asked out of the blue. Euphemia was shocked, then suddenly she became angry and feisty that her mother would think that.

"No, Mom, I am not!" Euphemia shouted.

"How can you say that?" Almasi shook her head. "Are you trying to deny the reality?"

Euphemia kept quiet and didn't utter a word. She wasn't sure what the truth was. Even if she was pregnant, she didn't want to confront it. Euphemia was too frightened to know the answer to constant mood changes. Finally, Almasi sighed and left her daughter so that she would gather her thoughts.

***

After being questioned by her mother, Euphemia decided to do a pregnancy test. Both Tabithi and herself went to the pharmacy and bought the test and went back home. Tabithi paced back and forth, restless, even though he was ready for a family. Therefore he was not surprised when Euphemia mentioned that she wanted to take a pregnancy test. He told her that he knew she could be pregnant because he had seen the way she was behaving the past few weeks. Her constant mood swings and change in habits gave it away.

Thabiti did not want to ask her, scared that it could turn out as putting pressure on her. He was waiting for Euphemia to really acknowledge the reality. He remained calm and collected but was getting anxious about the test results.

Euphemia walked out of the bedroom toward Thabiti. In her hands was the pregnancy strip that would reveal the truth behind her moods and not feeling well. She stood in front of him, tears brimming in her eyes, and slowly said, "I am pregnant."

Thabiti stilled, pondering at her declaration, "You-You...," he paused. "Are you serious, Euph?" His face turned pale; unshed tears were visible in his eyes.

"Am I?" He gulped. "Am I really going to be a dad?"

Euphemia nodded. Enthusiastic, he lifted her up in his arms and spun her around. Their living room was

Chapter 8

filled with the couple's laughter and tears of joy. Placing her down, he pulled her closer to him and kissed her passionately.

"I love you, Euph," he mumbled against her lips.
"I love you too," she murmured back.
However, while Thabiti was excited, Euphemia was fretting inside about the pregnancy. She was indeed happy, but she feared how things would go as she was still in her last year of college.

***

Euphemia took some time to go visit her mother "I know you're pregnant," Almasi uttered on another occasion. This time she was sure that her daughter was pregnant. Euphemia sighed, knowing she couldn't deny the truth forever even if she tried to.

"I'm pregnant," she murmured.

Almasi stared at her daughter for a minute, not because she was angry but because she didn't know what to do anymore. She was worried for her daughter; she wanted to find out everything so that she could calm her mind.

"Who is the father?" Almasi asked, placing a hand on her daughter's. "Do you know this man, Euph?"

"Yes, Mom, I know him," Euphemia mumbled. "Even Ivy knows about him."

"Ivy?" Almasi inquired, alarmed. "How does she

know about him?"

"When she went back with me as I went back to college one time during her high school break, she met him."

"What is his name? How did you two meet?"

"His...his name is Thabiti. We met when I was in my third year, and he works at a bank in my college town."

"Does he know about this?" inquired her mother.

"Yes, Mom, he knows. He's actually very excited for the baby." Euphemia flushed, thinking about how Thabiti had reacted. Almasi was watching her daughter keenly; she could see that whoever this 'man' was made her daughter happy.

As if realizing something, Euphemia took her mother's hands in hers and said, "Mom, Thabiti is a very good man." She paused, pondering on how to convince her mother to give her blessings. She didn't want to upset anyone, especially Almasi. "He's a very good person; he works in the bank. He's been taking care of me, and he's ready to take care of the baby too."

Almasi gazed at her daughter—really looking at her. It was the first time that she had acknowledged that her little Euphemia had grown up. Her daughter was finally going to be a mother—a 'title' that Almasi was proud of when she became pregnant with Euphemia. It

Chapter 8

brought tears to Almasi's eyes, knowing that Euphemia was on the way to starting her own family.

"Alright," Almasi uttered softly. "If that's what you think is right for you and if that's what you want, then I will support you. I will be there all the way."

"Thank you, Mom!" Euphemia exclaimed, giving her mother a warm and hearty hug. Almasi gladly reciprocated the hug and affection.

***

Almasi had a way of hiding so many of her feelings, and Euphemia believed she did that just to protect her children. When she realized Euphemia was pregnant, she already knew. It was a mother's instinct that made her conclude so. Almasi had already learned that Euphemia's husband had a good job, was loving, caring, and ready to continue paying for her daughter's remaining one year of college education.

Euphemia would see it in her mother's eyes that she was worried. However, Almasi had carefully thought this out and that she believed in her daughter because she raised her, knowing that if Euphemia had put her mind to do something, she would do it. Almasi knew she had given her children a good education, and she wanted them to be independent, especially Euphemia. Almasi herself was a hardworking and independent mother who took care of five children all by herself.

Euphemia thought that her mother was worried that she would not have a foundation where she would be an independent woman with her own financial backing. However, in her heart and mind, Euphemia believed she knew that hard times would come and pass and she would pursue her education and finish it—which she did and did not let her mother down.

The other thing that troubled Almasi was that as a mother, she wished that her children would be married, then become parents. However, by Kenyan common law Euphemia and Thabiti were already married even though they did not have formal paperwork to show that they were.

***

Euphemia was not surprised that she was pregnant, but it made her anxious. Her mind would wander around questioning herself:

Oh, what will happen next!

How am I going to make ends meet?

Will I be able to take care of the baby?

Euphemia was still in college; she was going to continue her semester while going through pregnancy. She feared what her classmates, friends, and teacher thought. The thought of their vicious stares and whispered rumors scared her. Thabiti could see her demotivation and being upset; he would encourage Euphemia with:

"I do not care what anyone has to say. It's our

Chapter 8

child. Nobody, and I mean, NOBODY has the right to talk about you or judge us," he would say, hugging her to himself. "Just ignore them and live your life as you want. We are happy, and that's what really matters, love." Thabiti's encouraging words were what made it easier for Euphemia. She knew someone loved her regardless of what everyone said—especially her classmates in college. Euphemia was nervous and confused.

She was excited about the new life that was growing inside her, but she also feared what the future was bringing. She didn't want her child to suffer because of her; she wanted to give everything. It was what made her troubled and indecisive. However, as time passed, she accepted the change, and along with her husband, they both worked hard to make ends meet.

***

Euphemia felt safe until her bump started to show, and she became nervous about attending college. She knew she needed to look after herself and the baby and would not be if she continued to worry. For the last few months before her delivery, Euphemia worked tirelessly hard to ensure she finished all her classes. She wanted to have only her final exam left after delivery. She believed that way would allow her enough time to take care of the new baby and finish school.

However, the thing that worried her was that she would not be working. Tabithi would have to carry the load of caring for the family. This made her anxious especially as the delivery date came closer. Tabithi noticed that Euphemia was anxious and he calmly asked if she was okay.

"What is wrong, darling?" Thabiti commented, gazing at his wife's troubled face. "You look worried."

"Thabiti…," Euphemia trailed off, glancing at her husband. "I don't know how we will take care of everything."

"What do you mean? Is something wrong? Are you hurt somewhere?"

"I am just…."

"Euph," Thabiti mumbled, leaning in and taking her face in his hands. He looked at her adoringly. "You can tell me anything, love. I am here to support and love you. And I promise we will make it work."

Euphemia stared into his eyes, only to find assurance and love in them. She gained confidence with it and told him everything that had been troubling her. After she was done, she felt like the burden on her shoulders had been lifted.

"Oh, Euph!" He exclaimed, chuckling and stroking her face. "You don't have to worry about anything, babe. I have figured out everything already. Remember, I have a job!"

Euphemia ceased talking when she realized something. "Wait for a second, but how will you manage my college fees?"

Chapter 8

"Hey, hey, hey." He kissed her lips slowly. "For me now, you and our baby are the top priority, alright? I have to provide for you both."

Thabiti was true to his promise; he continued working at a bank and supporting the family. He supported his wife through her final year of college and even paid her school fees.

He treated Euphemia like his child; he ensured he woke her up, prepared her breakfast, and then he would drive her to the college. There was nothing Euphemia would have asked for in life than for a man that loved her so much that he gave and continued to give and do anything for her.

Just a week before her delivery date, Euphemia dropped out of school to have the baby. It was a joyous moment for the couple when their daughter Faraja was born. After the delivery, Euphemia had to stay home with the baby for a few weeks before returning back to college to do her final exam. She walked to and from college and during her breaks would rush home to go and see and feed her baby. Euphemia's life was blissful; with her loving husband and baby.

Chapter 9 – Struggle is Real

"No person can become strong without struggle, without the effort of pitting himself against trouble and hardship. And to meet and deal with life creatively, we will always need to be alert and thoughtful and to think in a positive manner, constantly rallying personality forces into effective and desirable action."
~ Dr. Norman Vincent Peale, The Positive Principle Today

In life, at a point in time one will experience difficulties and challenges. We all will encounter issues no matter who we are, where we come from, or what we have in life. Stress undoubtedly makes one feel anxious and continuously prevents us from getting what we want or need. Each day brings challenges no matter how small but overcoming the challenges fosters endurance. Similarly, Euphemia was no exception.

***

One afternoon, while Euphemia was tending to Faraja,

Chapter 9

her phone rang. It was Thabiti.

"Hey, honey!" Euphemia said into the phone.

"Euph…" Thabiti trailed off and sighed.

"What is it?" she asked, alerted. "Did something happen?"

"They let me go, they fired me!," he told her, saddened.

"What? Are you serious?" Euphemia responded, shocked to the core. She became numb and speechless. The sound of Faraja crying made her come out of her reverie, and she realized her husband was still on the phone. "Euph? Euphemia?" Thabiti kept on asking. "Are you still there?"

"Yes, yes, I am still here," she uttered. "How did it happen? What was the reason behind it?"

"They said they are cutting down on staff and cutting hours so that the company can keep rolling," he sighed.

His unexpected phone call that evening was a harsh reminder to Euphemia that things did not always go as planned.

It took the couple a few weeks to gather themselves and their thoughts as life was not on hold' they still had a baby to care for and bills to be taken care of. After days of deliberating, they made some required changes. As the saying goes, easier said than done. As time went by, things became tough. It was difficult for Euphemia and Thabiti to provide for their family as they became mentally and emotionally exhausted. The couple, along with the baby, was forced to cut down on spending through the days ahead.

What kept them going was trusting and believing in God, the love, compassion, and trust they had in each other. Euphemia would comfort her little family, trying her best not to look worried or scared. Even if she had to hide her tears from her husband—she would. But in front of him, she would stay strong so that he could stay motivated.

"I am sorry, darling," Thabiti told his wife one day. "Because of me, you and Faraja are suffering. If only I could've done something. I don't know how to make things right."

"Honey, it is not your fault," Euphemia muttered, staring deep into his eyes. "There are many things in our life we had no clue of."

"But—but I promised you I will provide for you and the baby!" he stated. It shocked Euphemia as she had never seen her husband being this vulnerable.

"Thabiti, it's…it's alright. We will get through it." She pulled him closer and gave him a big hug. "We have each other, don't we?"

Chapter 9

Thabiti nodded, and Euphemia smiled at him. She said, "Now, what more do we need? When we are together, we can conquer every problem and hardship. I know we are going through really hard times right now, but one day, things will get better."

Thabiti gazed at her, pleased to know he had such a wonderful woman as his wife. Someone who understood him and stood with him no matter what. No matter the situation and no matter the hurdles they would face. "Thank you," he mumbled, kissing her. "Thank you for coming into my life and choosing me."

Euphemia smiled and kissed him back.

***

In those difficult times, Euphemia's family didn't leave her; they supported her through thick and thin—especially Almasi. She would pray for the couple and their child. God blessed the couple with one more child, a son. As Euphemia remembered, years after they all had grown up and now had their own, Almasi would worry about them and pray for their well-being. When it was hard for the couple to make ends meet, and the time when Euphemia's son fell sick, Alamsi really took her time to pray and fast for God to heal her daughter's son. Tabithi and his family never lost hope; they didn't let any hardship tear them apart!

Almasi had purposed in her heart and mind to pray for Faraja and all her children and grandchildren. Little did Euphemia realize or know her mother prophesied over their lives often. Almasi would get prophecies and write them down in a journal. One by one they came to pass as she said it would.

One day Almasi called Euphemia and told her God was going to heal her child and God was going to take her to higher places. Euphemia doubted that, considering what she and her family were going through at that time. She thought because Almasi was a mother, she was saying it just to reassure her. However, what happened after, surprised Euphemia.

Each one of the prophecies happened one by one, if Almasi's prophecies had become true. It amazed Euphemia t just as Almasi had predicted, the trajectory of her life continued to go higher. Euphemia knew God was not done with her yet. Her son stopped falling sick as frequently and continued to be in good health. Euphemia was thankful to God and would always continue to be grateful.

Almasi had given all her children Bibles while they were growing up. Euphemia still kept and read the same Bible her mother had given her—though it was a little bit worn. Euphemia kept telling herself she should repair it so she could keep it. She treasured it and read it as often as she could.

Euphemia was not good at reading the Bible daily, but she tried just like how her mother had taught her. The Bible was colored with highlighted verses. Most importantly, it continued to guide her through life.

Euphemia had tried to emulate her mother so she could

Chapter 9

pass the same way she knew God to her children. Even though she knew she could never fit exactly into how Almasi did it, she still tried. Euphemia always knew her mother's prayers helped her through life's difficult times. Euphemia soon found herself moving forward, and the tough time became easier. She realized she was closer to the peaceful life she had been praying for.

Chapter 10 – Blessed

"But blessed is the one who trusts in the LORD, whose confidence is in him. They will be like a tree planted by the water that sends out its roots by the stream. It does not fear when heat comes; its leaves are always green. It has no worries in a year of drought and never fails to bear fruit."
~ Jeremiah 17:7-8

From the day we are born until we become adults, our life isn't without suffering or hardships at a point in time. Life is also filled with times of happiness and joy. Any person's goal should be to strike a balance.

Everyone has goals, aspirations and objectives in life they hope to achieve and advance toward in the future. However, life may throw you a curveball. Do you remember times in your life that have left you so sad, frustrated and hopeless? Sometimes so sickening that

Chapter 10

food could not go down your throat and you started to lose so much weight?

Yes, life can get complicated, become mentally exhausting, and demotivating at times. Regardless, there is one thing we all need to know. Our lives can have a lovely balance. There can be times when we have peace and joy even in the worst of circumstances.

What we need to understand is that our goal in life is to advance, but sometimes we also have to retreat. Knowing that things always get better and work well for those who trust in God gave Euphemia courage. Furthermore, knowing so made Euphemia strive forward; and she never lost hope and always worked hard to get through tough times.

***

Remember Thabiti lost his banking job after Euphemia had just completed college and they had their first child Faraja. During that period of struggling to make ends meet he made a tough decision to have Euphemia and his child tentatively go live with her mother Almasi. Meanwhile, he decided to move to the city to start living with his brother because the city is where he would be able to find a job. He stayed in the city for a little while, but he painfully missed his family.

Thabiti's brother was kind enough and willing to sacrifice his space and allowed Thabiti to bring his family to live in his home. Tabithi's brother was well off with a great attitude. He was very kind and down to earth a better example of his character is to say he was very humble.

He offered Thabiti to bring his family over because he did not want his brother to be separated from his family. Thabiti went and got his wife and daughter from Euphemia's parents' home. His family now had accommodation at his brother's house, including all the help they needed.

God has always been good; it did not take long when Euphemia finally got her first job as a nurse that was well paying. After some time, Euphemia and Thabiti moved into their own home. The house wasn't a luxurious one but a small comfortable one. It didn't matter to them if it wasn't as good as they would have wanted it to be. The couple was happy at least they had shelter, food on the table, and were able to pay their bills.

When they had moved in, Euphemia and Thabiti didn't have many possessions with them or money. They had to buy everything from scratch, even a mattress. And as they couldn't afford luxurious items, they were happy with the bare minimum they could manage to pay for. That was all the couple had.

The couple had a mattress and a cooking stove. They decided to sleep on the same mattress, Euphemia, Thabiti, and Faraja. When life got better, they managed to get help from a house worker to help care for Faraja and with house chores as Tabithii and Euphemia now had jobs to go to.

Life was still not easy for both Euphemia and Thabiti but the love they had for one another is what kept them going. Days and months went by, and Euphemia

Chapter 10

continued to go to work as a nurse. She had managed to secure a job and was pleased to provide for her family. Some weeks later, Thabiti ended up finding a job in the industrial area.

He had been working hard for months, trying to find a good and stable job. He would wake up early to look for jobs and work contract jobs during the day. Thabiti didn't lose hope; even if he didn't get hired, he would run errands for anyone just so he could bring home something to his family.

Days turned to months, and the couple continued working. As years went by, Euphemia and Thabiti moved into a cheaper house that had one more room for the kids and was sufficient for them. Thabiti got a job as a public transportation driver 'Matatu driver.' That's when things got back to normal, and Euphemia's life was back to normal. It was then God blessed them with their second child.

Euphemia and Thabiti were overjoyed when they heard about the news. It was like a flower had bloomed into their thorny life. It didn't matter to them if they had to struggle and things were exhausting for them. They felt happy they were blessed with a baby boy. The couple named their second born Bahati.

Euphemia and Thabiti tried the best they could to provide for their children. They denied themselves everything so that their children could go to a private school. Eventually, when they had earned enough, they decided to admit Bahati and Faraja into the school. They sent their son and daughter to a private school. Euphemia continued to work as a nurse while looking after her family.

***

Euphemia didn't let her mother's teaching go to waste. She wanted to teach her children about God just like how she and her siblings were taught. As her children grew up, she bought Bibles for both of them. Each day, she encouraged them to read the Bible and pray. Sometimes Euphemia felt like they thought it was just a routine chore and were not taking it seriously. She didn't want that for her children.

She would tell them every night when she was about to go to bed:

"Please pray and read your Bibles," Euphemia said as she hugged them and gave them a kiss. Looking at them with a beautiful smile on her face, she would tell them, "I love you, Bahati and Faraja."

Euphemia also taught them to trust in God and literally call on Jesus in situations they could not speak or handle. If an instance or events happened in their lives and Euphemia realized or saw there was something going on in their lives, her children would exclaim, "Jesus!" or "Lord!"

Euphemia was thankful that they knew there was a God that existed, and she was thankful to her mother for teaching that to her also. She was glad and now is able to teach that to her children. Whenever Euphemia looked

Chapter 10

back at her life and all the things that had happened—the events, the incidents—there was no way she could have gotten this far and continue living her life without God. She would not have had a happy, loving, and healthy family, were it not for God's grace and mercy.

Euphemia knew if it was not for her mother's prayers and instilling the fear of God in her life, she couldn't have made it this far. She would have given up hope and continued to fall apart and away from what life and happiness is. Euphemia continued to live her life peacefully while praying and hoping that she would instill the same moral values into her children.

She hoped that she was creating or extending a hope into the future that Bahati and Faraja would instill the same legacy into their children and their children's children. She prayed her lineage would continue to know God and know how He is so good to them!

Chapter 11 – Coming to America

"Life might be difficult for a while, but I would tough it out because living in a foreign country is one of those things that everyone should try at least once. My understanding was that it completed a person, sanding down the rough provincial edges and transforming you into a citizen of the world."
~ David Sedaris

Typically, individuals go abroad for a myriad of reasons, including business, improved security, or the chance to live a better life. Providing your family with better opportunities such as housing, education and many other things also top the list. There are those who shuffle back and forth to their home country and the foreign country, and then those who decide to permanently relocate to a new place.

With the change of country, the persons and their families way of living may change. An individual's way

Chapter 11

of living alters in some ways as a result of their relocation to a new country. They learn and adjust to new customs, traditions, and laws. This was what Euphemia and her family experienced when they first moved. Her simple but tough life took a unique turn when they moved, for the better.

***

One morning when Euphemia received a call from her sister, Ivy. Euphemia would've never thought that a simple call could shift her life dynamics so much. Euphemia didn't know she would get a call from immigration about papers she never submitted.

They told her that her papers had been approved for a green card, it is now time to start working on the green card process. What is going on? she thought, gazing at the landline phone. When did I apply for the green card? Did someone do it on my behalf? Or Is this a prank?

Euphemia was confused; she couldn't understand what was happening. How and from where did the sudden change come into her life? Her mind was going hazy. It wasn't until Ivy called and asked her about the 'green card approval' that Euphemia realized everything. Without her knowledge, Ivy had applied for a green card lottery for entry into The United States of America.

"What?" Euphemia shrieked, flabbergasted.

"But—but how and why?"

"I…I didn't like seeing you people suffer," Ivy confessed. "It was distressing for me to see you and your family struggle. I want to see you happy, Euphemia! It's the least I could have done for you."

"Oh, Ivy!" Euphemia sighed and rubbed her forehead, with nervous energy. "I—I don't know what to say anymore. You shouldn't have."

"Yes!" I should have Ivy insisted, "You are my only Sister I had to!"

She didn't know what to feel anymore; she was so happy, glad someone cared for her as her sister did. Euphemia never liked to burden anyone—not even her siblings. When Thabiti came back from work, Euphemia told him everything. He was so overwhelmed with joy. The couple broke down crying, feeling blessed and cherished in that moment together.

After some time passed, they received Euphemia's green card and they began making travel arrangements. Euphemia was the first one to travel to the United States as she was the bearer of the green card. She arrived in the country in mid October.

To date, she remembers it was a cold winter morning when her flight landed. It was an awe-struck moment for her when she saw the fascinating sun shining from the airplane window.

"Oh my God!" She exclaimed to herself. "It is so beautiful! I have never seen such an amazing sight!" Then

Chapter 11

she sighed. "Thabiti, Bahati, and Faraja would've loved it!" She was picked from the airport by Tabithi's family, her in-laws. The drive home was spectacular, the scenery, the different cars, the traffic were all so different and perplexing.

The next day, the morning chill enthralled her. Euphemia would walk out of the house dressed in a simple T-shirt and shorts. Even though the frosty wind would hit her as soon as she crossed the threshold, she was excited to step out of the house; she still could not believe it. The view and the atmosphere were great.

Euphemia missed her husband and children deeply. She was alone in a foreign country, away from her husband and children for the first time. It was a new, exciting experience, but a lonely one for her.

Whenever she saw or experienced something astounding, she felt bad her family was missing out. She wanted Thabiti and their kids to experience the best moments too. Euphemia would often tell herself,
"It's okay, Euphemia. It is just a matter of months, and they will be here with me. All I need is a little patience and a lot of willpower to bear the wait."

A month passed by in a blink, and Thabiti followed her, arriving in the United States. The couple was happy to be united; however, they felt incomplete without their children. It took a longer time for their kids to join them.

It was painful and hard for both the parents and

children. Euphemia and Thabiti worried about their well-being. Even though they knew Faraja and Bahati were in good hands, they couldn't help but be concerned about them.

If only it was easy for all of them to have traveled together. More months passed by, and finally, it was the time everyone was looking forward to all of them being together. On one fine day the following year in February, Baraka and Faraja arrived in the United States.

Oh, what a happy day—when Euphemia's family was reunited. The tears of joy that flowed from their eyes expressed their longing and love for each other.

Euphemia and her family started living with a cousin of hers in a beautiful subdivision in a bungalow. Her family was offered one bedroom as their own to reside. Life wasn't easy for them in such a tight place, but they were beyond grateful. It was a sacrifice that Tabithi's cousin had made and really his family too. He didn't live alone prior to them moving there.

Euphemia and Thabiti knew that they had a time limit before they would naturally wear out the generous invitation. Their plan was to make use of every moment to find jobs, work hard, save, and get their own place. This is nothing new, but required for them to have a successful life in the future, especially in this country.

***

The home Euphemia's family resided in fortunately had an old computer the family was barely using.

Chapter 11

They were kind enough to allow Euphemia to use the computer to process her work programs to return to work as a nurse. She also knew she was required to do credential evaluation for her nursing school transcripts and sit for the American Nursing Entrance Test. She had to pass the exam before she could start working in this country.

It was not easy for her; transitioning into a new country wasn't easy as she thought One of Euphemia's colleagues told her t she could reach for help when she and her family landed in the states. It was him who reminded her that her wish to come to the United States had come true.

"Do you remember the time in college when you talked about going to America?" Evelyn asked. "Now look at you now, Euph, you are here!"

"Really?" Euphemia had asked, puzzled. "I don't remember saying that."

It made her acknowledge how important it was to speak into her future and dreams really matter. Sometimes people will say something just in a passing way. They didn't even ponder on it much. However, through prayer, hard work, and pushing towards your vision and goals, it can be achieved.

As a nurse, Euphemia had set her mind to preparing to relocate to work in Britain. Nonetheless, she was lucky that whatever program she was working on her paperwork for working in the United States or the UK.

was about the same. So starting this process in the United States made it a little easier for her to continue the process someday in the UK.

It was sort of easy for Euphemia to get working on her certification to do list. It was simple because she knew what to do and started studying for the English Exam immediately. Euphemia continued using the computer to start preparing for credential evaluation. She studied day and night for the English exam to ease her fears.

She feared she would fail. Weeks turned into months, and Euphemia sat for the nursing exam and failed the exam the first time. Euphemia would have given up if it wasn't for Thabiti's encouragement and support. He was there for her throughout, doing as much as he could to help her.

With her husband's love and support, Euphemia tried again and took the exam a second time. It turned out to be the best decision of her life! Her first attempt failed miserably; however, the second time, she passed.

"Thabiti!" Euphemia shouted. "Thabiti! Where are you?"

"What's wrong? Why are you shouting?" Thabiti asked, running into the living room. "Did something happen?"

"Yes! I passed the exam!" she told him excitedly.

"What! Really?" he inquired, just as excited as

Chapter 11

she was. When Euphemia nodded, he pulled her in for a warm hug. "I knew you could do it, my love."

"It's all because of you!" Her eyes began filling with tears.

"If it wasn't for your unconditional love and help, I don't think I could—"

Thabiti placed a lingering kiss on her mouth, shutting her off from over thinking about what was to come next. She could see the love in his eyes and she reciprocated his love as they leaned back and smiled at each other.

"You don't need to thank me, sweetheart." He smiled at her fondly and stroked her cheek, wiping the tears that had rolled down her cheek. "I didn't do anything. It was all you, my darling wife, your hard work, perseverance and persistence."

Euphemia smiled at him, hugging the love of her life tighter.

Things began to line up for the couple. Their blessings were just around the corner, seemingly waiting for them. Initially Euphemia couldn't work as a nurse because she had to have had the credential evaluated, and pass the English test and the Nursing Test. Prior to that, the only job she could work was at a grocery store. So, she began her life in the U.S by working in a Walmart for almost two years.

***

When they moved to the states, Euphemia and her family went through financial hardship like any other newly immigrated family trying to build a foundation. They found it hard, trying to look for independence and balance.

Neither Euphemia nor Thabiti wanted to become a burden and bother to anyone. They didn't want to outstay their visit and comfort in someone else's home. Therefore, being forced to rush towards getting into a new apartment puts incredible pressure on them, but two strings tied together are definitely stronger than one. Thabiti and Euphemia worked hard to make it possible to move into their new home.

Nevertheless, they didn't let disappointments and failures set them back. The couple was strong, even if they had to try again and again; they would. It was their immense hard work and persistence that made Euphemia and Thabiti continue forging ahead.

***

As an overnight shelf stocker, Euphemia was used to working overnight shifts. There wasn't any trouble with her schedule, but them not being in a position to purchase a vehicle. Thabiti's cousin would let him borrow his car from time to time to be of help. Euphemia didn't know how to drive the car because it was a manual.

Sometimes she would walk to or from work late at night whenever her husband was not available; or when they did not have access to the car. While she was work-

Chapter 11

ing in Walmart, she earned almost $200 a week. Her husband was working at a store that was owned by a family member but was not earning much.

In Kenya, drivers drive on the left side of the road and the cars are right hand drive. Therefore driving on the right side of the street in the US for Tabithi was something he had to always remember. The transition wasn't easy for Thabiti; he struggled to maintain the rules of the road. But over the course of time, he learned it and became the 'best driver' among his peers.

Euphemia and Thabiti managed to save $800 after a few months. They thought that was a lot of money to pay for a down payment for a used car. As they had no clue about the car dealers in the new country, they asked Tabithi's cousin for help. He took them to several dealerships with his wife and children in tow.

Their first encounter was not shaping up too great. It felt like all day they sat at the car dealer's shop. The car dealer kept showing them cars that were not in good condition. It was disappointing and upsetting for Euphemia and Thabit to sit there.

It was now six o'clock in the evening; and the family had not eaten and still the $800 sat in their pocket. Euphemia and Thabiti were clueless as to what was going to happen.

After what seemed like hours, somebody sent them to a different car dealer. The car dealership sent an employee to come and pick them up, telling Euphemia and Thabiti that they had a car over there.

"Is it okay?" Euphemia asked. "Will we be safe? He is a complete stranger, Thabiti."

"I don't know," Thabiti mumbled and then looked at her. "But trust me, and don't worry, I won't let anyone harm you."

"Alright," Euphemia mumbled. "I believe in you, Thabiti."

Euphemia was frightened; she knew they were dealing with a stranger. They didn't know this person and were trusting him enough to get into the car. The whole ride was tense and terrifying for her. She kept praying for her and her family's lives. They were only able to relax when they arrived at the other car dealer's place.

Phew! Euphemia sighed and thought. Thank God! The car dealer showed them six different cars, all of which were in poor condition. Luckily Tabithi was familiar with cars and he was able to determine which car was best. After going through all the cars, Tabithi finally found the one which was in fairly good condition, and the best for their price range. The car was a manual! God is so good, Thabiti knew how to drive it already.

"Thabiti," she murmured, eyes fixated on the vehicle.

"Yes, darling?" Thabiti inquired.

"Is it good? She asked worriedly. He glanced at

Chapter 11

her and said, "It's the best for what and the condition is better than the others. We have no other choice," he said. The vehicle was a popular American black car and it was a small size—

Thabiti asked the car dealer if he could drive the car around a little bit for a test drive. The car dealer agreed, and with Euphemia and the children in the car, Thabiti drove it around the dealer's place.

"This is the best we can have," Euphemia said. "Yes, you are right," Thabiti replied. Turning toward the car dealer, he said, "We'll take it."

The paperwork was completed within an hour, and the couple took the car. At that time, they didn't have a smartphone. They asked the dealer to print directions for them to get home. While Euphemia read the directions, "Take a right here, and a left and at the light," her husband drove as she navigated through the dark of night in areas they had never been before.

It was only by God's grace they arrived home safely. Their children were tired and hungry. The family ate and showered, prayed and thanked God for seeing them through the day and blessing them up to that point.

Months went by, and Euphemia continued working at night. They were able to get a nearby apartment to Walmart and convenient for Thabiti's job as well. Euphemia still had to walk from time to time to get to work even after buying the car. Thabiti had a job in Atlanta, which was about thirty miles away from their residence.

Euphemia would leave the house at ten o'clock at night and walk to Walmart.

It would be dark and scary for her, especially when sometimes there was no one on the street. The scariest part was that Euphemia would occasionally encounter snakes on the pathway! It continued on for months until she was able to pass her nursing exam. That day did not come a moment too soon.

***

After Euphemia passed her exam, she got a job in a city hospital in Atlanta. Her job was forty miles away from where they lived. The only problem was that she had to drive to work and she didn't know how to do that. While working at Walmart, her husband dropped and picked her up or she would commute by taxi or walking. Euphemia was lucky one day, a new employee started at Walmart who fortunately was from her home country. The man was kind enough to offer to teach her how to drive, she and her husband thought.

Thabiti had tried to teach his wife how to drive the manual car, but it was so difficult for Euphemia and she gave up on trying to learn. It was a disaster as both Tabithi's and Euphemia's anxiety or frustration ended up having them on the outs. They were not able to work together on the driving issue–no matter how much they loved each other.

So, Euphemia's only choice was for the nice gentleman at her workplace to teach her. Paying someone was out of the question and not even a consideration.

Chapter 11

He was so kind and taught her how to drive during their break times and after work. Gradually with time, she learned how to drive.

When Euphemia had learned how to drive, the couple went on to get a second new car. They went to the dealership, and they saw a Honda Odyssey.

It was a nice, new van to add to the family.

Yes! Tabithi said, Now you can drive yourself to and from work. You must be the one to take the van for a test drive. Euphemia was anxious at the same time excited, and it brought a smile to Thabiti's face. Euphemia got into the driver's seat while the car dealer got onto the passenger side, Thabiti along with their children got into the back. Euphemia drove the van safely all the way to a park which was nearby.

However, when they were coming out of the park, her mind switched off back to the Kenyan driving way and she started driving on the left side of the Road! Euphemia didn't know why and how it happened. She—to this date—couldn't recall why her mind drifted as she was so intentional on driving on the right side of the road.

For the first few seconds when she turned onto the main road she in her mind was confident she was driving on the required side. Euphemia was driving confidently, when suddenly she saw a car coming toward her. Her children began screaming, and her eyes bulged out of their sockets in shock. She could hear everyone's shout of horror. "Mom! Mom! You are driving on the wrong side", she had her children screaming.

The driver in the oncoming car moved towards the opposite side which was the wrong side to try and escape from colliding into her. Quickly, Euphemia realized she was driving on the wrong side and steered the car back to the correct side of the road. Interestingly, the car dealer staff sitting next to Euphemia on the passenger seat did not utter a word or even help redirect Euphemia. It was a frightening experience. Scared and austruck, shaking, her husband and children were concerned if she was okay.

"Mom!" the children said and her husband, "Euphemia!"

Thabiti and the kids tried to get her attention. She slowly came to and replied, "I am okay!" Euphemia exclaimed and turned around to look at them. "Are you all alright?"

"Yes, we are," Thabiti said and nodded along with the children. After that incident, it took a lot of courage for Euphemia to familiarize herself with the roads. She would drive on the street with a friend or a colleague to memorize the place and the area. And once she knew how, Euphemia would drive around everywhere by herself.

As time progressed, Euphemia continued working as a nurse, her husband for a food production company, and their children continued going to school. The family decided it was time to advance beyond the apartment

Chapter 11

and move into a new home with God's grace and mercy. It was exciting and a great reward for their hard work of making a living in a new country; and it would help them call America home.

Chapter 12 – Heartbreaking Land Events

"Life might be difficult for a while, but I would tough it out because living in a foreign country is one of those things that everyone should try at least once. My understanding was that it completed a person, sanding down the rough provincial edges and transforming you into a citizen of the world."
~ David Sedaris

One Day Euphemia learned that her father had started selling the land that Almasi and her children had lived on from the time they were born to adults. The several acres of land that she had tilled, plowed, planted, and harvested over the years to feed, clothe, and educate them was now in jeopardy. She knew it was being threatened with the thought of losing her home.

Almasi was a well educated woman who had worked her way through the ranks, gaining knowledge from the many people in society she knew. Almasi was

Chapter 12

well equipped with information on her children's right to matrimonial land. She feared she and her children would be kicked out of their home, and she couldn't possibly stop fighting for their rights.

Almasi knew her husband was a man who was also well educated, prideful, as well as egotistical and would do anything to make her life difficult and unbearable. Possibly push her to the brim of giving up on fighting to keep part of the land. Of all the years he knew her, and he always intentionally underestimated her.

"I won't give up fighting and let you sell my land!" Almasi told Barasa. "It's my children's right, and you're not going to leave them without a home and land they rely on to sustain their wellbeing and education."

Almasi went to court to fight for her land for her children. And it soon turned into an extended family battle, as most of the family members, Euphemia's aunties and uncles were furious. They didn't like that Almasi was going to court with the land issue. One beautiful evening some of Euphemia's half brothers and sisters came to Euphemi's home unexpected and uninvited. Instead of coming into the house like anyone could, they marched straight to the farm where Almasi had planted sugarcane and other plants for commercial and home purposes. They began cutting down the sugarcane and eating it, while shouting at the top of their voices" farming Almasi's house.`

They went on to chant, "It is our father's land." The stepsiblings threatened Alamasi and her children.

"There's nothing you can do. If he wants to sell it, he can sell it! So, stop this foolishness of taking him to court and threatening him!"

Almasi's youngest son's Ezra and Zion were then adults and they decided to confront Barasa. Their father decided to have the police arrest them and take them to jail. A court case was opened between Barasa and Almasi for some time and the fight waged on. Almas had since retired and therefore It wasn't easy for her financially to keep paying the fees and care for her youngest children still persuing college.

The court cases went on for years until the court decided to give Almasi 25 acres of land and the house. Barasa got the rest of the land which God knows what he later did with it. A story for another time when my father did not cease to disappoint and be a cruel man hell bent on destroying my mother.

Even though everything was sorted out and Almasi got her land while Barasa got his, the extended family did not take everything well. They said things like: "She is a bad woman because she fought her husband to get land."

"How can she go to court?"

"She doesn't care about her family's reputation."

"Almasi isn't a good wife!"

"Doesn't she think about her husband's image?"

Chapter 12

Almasi's life had never been a bed of roses, her marriage was a disaster except for being blessed by having beautiful children. It wasn't really easy, actually it was tormenting to say the least. Even in her retirement period—after her children had grown up and gone their own way, she was still fighting for her life. Fighting for what she had worked for all her life.

Almasi got the land and then divided it amongst her sons and daughters—equally. She was a firm believer that every child should be treated the same way, whether a boy or a girl. Unfortunately she never lived to see the title deeds of the land, she died the same day the title deed was processed and delivered. To date all her children remain forever grateful for the persistence and endurance their mother gave into ensuring her children were cared for even into her death.

Chapter 13 – From Sickness to Death

"But there's a story behind everything. How a picture got on a wall. How a scar got on your face. Sometimes the stories are simple, and sometimes they are hard and heartbreaking. But behind all your stories is always your mother's story because hers is where yours begin."
~ Mitch Albom

Have you ever experienced the loss of either both or one of your parents? How did you cope with their death? Was the grief of their loss so much that you found it hard to comprehend it?

It can be challenging to approach the topic of grief and loss. However, losing your parents, who are the foundation and basically the most significant people in our lives can be extremely devastating. When we are born, the first people we see after the medical team if being delivered in a hospital are our parents. Our basic needs, such

Chapter 13

as nourishment, livelihood, and clothing, depend upon them.

Our first impressions of the universe and what it holds or has prepared for us are constituted through our relationships and reflections with our parents. Even though we know that everyone in life is destined eventually to pass away; still losing our parents—the people who raised us—can be a very painful event. An honest feeling is that we are never ready to say goodbye to our parents. Similarly, the shocking news of her mother's illness broke Euphemia's heart.

***

Two years later, after Euphemia had bought her own house, Almasi got sick. She heard from her siblings her mother had gotten very sick and was having to go see the doctors every so often. Euphemia was not surprised to later learn that her mother was battling some kind of illness but certainly did not disclose it to her children because she didn't want to worry them. Like she always did in troubled times before, she wanted to protect her family as best as possible. The love she had for her children always wanted her to make them believe everything was okay.

Never at any time during her childrens' childhood, teenage and young adulthood did Almasi's children see their mother visit the doctor. She never laid down in the bed sick or even got admitted to the hospital. To learn of her now needing the doctors in the prime of their lives was shocking and fearful to speak the least.

Euphemia's mind was spinning around. How did this happen? She thought. When did mother become ill? Have I been too busy to notice, and does she know how much I care?

As Euphemia tried to comprehend her mother's condition, there were times she remembered and thought about how her mother worked so hard farming and rearing cattle for commercial purposes to make money for their futures easily came to mind. Alamasi would say she does it all for them. Euphemia, being honest, would say her mother's illness was not a recent onset; she had shown signs of being sick for years.

Almasi was unwell way back when her children were younger Euphemia recalled. However, she didn't let her children know she was suffering. She continued working and fighting for her children's rights without informing them what was wrong with her.

In those years, Almasi had never complained about her condition. Whenever the mother-daughter would have a conversation, Almasi didn't tell her daughter her problems. She was such a selfless person who wanted the best for everyone around her.

Maybe she didn't want to worry me? Euphemia had thought. She knew I was going through tough times myself.

Euphemia using her Nursing knowledge from the symptoms and signs were being explained to her by her siblings, was that she probably had congestive heart fail-

Chapter 13

ure or Chronic obstructive pulmonary disease (COPD). She was upset her mother was going through some medical condition and she couldn't be there to support her. Nonetheless, she thought Almasi would get better and recover soon. If only Euphemia had known the reality was far from her positive outlook. Her life would change yet again…

***

Euphemia had wanted her mother to come and live with her in the United States. She had already filed for Almasi's green card. However, the process was taking too long. She feared her mother's condition could deteriorate before she would make it to the United States to live with her.

"Don't worry, Euphemia," Thabiti told her one day. "She will get better."

"I cannot understand what is happening," Euphemia said, sighing. "She was doing good when I talked to her last week, and now, she is going through tests after tests, and having to visit the doctors and get admitted more often than usual."

"I know it is a difficult time, but now I am here with you." her loving husband replied. Euphemia smiled, glad to know that she had her husband's support. Being in America for so long, Euphemia and Thabiti knew it would be hard for them to book a flight as they were expensive.

It was difficult for them to travel to Kenya to visit

Almasi at that time. They had arrived in the country in 2006, and still, in 2014, the couple was barely making ends meet. Traveling at a time like this was out of the picture. Thabiti did not have a really well-paying job; they were just barely making it.

"What should we do?" Euphemia asked. "We can't possibly travel right now."

"Hmm," Thabiti mumbled, thinking. "How about instead of traveling, we send money for her treatment, admission, and medications?"

"I think…I think that will be better." She nodded her head.

"I know, darling, you want to be with your mother." He sighed, heartbroken they couldn't do more for Euphemia and her mother. "Let's save money, so we are able to visit her."

Euphemia and Thabiti could not make any travel plans, but they continuously spoke to her on the phone. Euphemia was restless; she was unable to think clearly, knowing that her mother wasn't well and possibly dying. Her husband noticed her distress and he would try to comfort her. He knew she was worried and wanted to be there with Almasi. One day, when Thabiti came back from work, he surprised her with a gift.

"What? How?" Euphemia exclaimed, gazing at the ticket.

Chapter 13

"I saved up money so you could go visit her," Thabiti told her.

"Oh, My God!" She began crying. "Thank you so much, Thabiti!"

"Seriously? Am I really going to see my mom?" He shook his head. "Yes darling, I know you were concerned for her, and it's the least I can do right now. So don't worry about anything and go."

Thabiti gave everything he had to ensure that Euphemia's mother was well taken care of. He even took out some money from his savings to send his wife to Kenya to visit her sick mother.

***

In 2012, Almasi had been checking in and out of the hospital due to severe pain and weakness. When she visited the doctors, most of the time, they would tell her it was malaria or typhoid. They weren't willing to appropriately run tests and diagnostics, they only speculated it as a psychological condition and diagnosed Almasi as such. Almasi did not struggle with a mental condition, she was strong, didn't complain, and was very sane; the doctors got that very wrong.

It wasn't until Euphemia and her siblings probed and intervened that the doctors went ahead and did some tests. It was then that they learned that Almasi had cancer. She was diagnosed with multiple myeloma.

The news came as a shock to the family. They

couldn't believe Almasi was going through something so severe, and the pain was excruciating yet she bore it all that time. The siblings knew it was difficult to get their mother treated.

Unfortunately, in third-world countries like Kenya, diagnosing cancer was a long shot at that time. And by the time the doctor diagnosed her, it was already late. The cancer was in stage three or four. The hardest thing was even the doctors couldn't tell whether it was stage three or stage four.

It was sadly concluded that the survival chance of Almasi was zero due to late cancer findings and her short management window. During that time, Euphemia was able to visit her mother twice. The first time she took her mother to the doctor and listened to the doctor talk about psychological issues. The second time was when Almasi was going through chemotherapy. Alamasi was moved to a city hospital where she got admitted for management of multiple myeloma. Euphemia traveled to be with her mother for a few weeks when she was able to take off work.

Throughout that time, Euphemia visited with her mother in the hospital daily. She went in the morning and spent the day with her to ensure she ate, asked questions to get clarification from the doctors, and to find out how her treatment was progressing.

Euphemia took several pictures with her mother and spent intimate and quality time with her. As she prepared to get back to the US she left feeling a little better

Chapter 13

that her mother felt and looked better but she knew that progressively she would get worse because the doctors now wanted to have her stop chemotherapy. It wasn't working to stop the progression of the disease and they wanted to begin radiation. Reluctant Almasi decided she wanted to go back home, there was nowhere she could live in the city so she had to go back to the hometown where she lived.

Unfortunately Euphemia had to travel back to the US but her heart was heavy because she knew she may not ever see her mother alive again. It was difficult for Euphemeia, but again she had to travel back to work. The money she had she needed to use to go back to the U.S. and also provide care for her mother. Whenever Euphemia called back home to check on her mother's condition, they would tell her, "She's okay; she is fine." Her heart and mind wanted desperately to believe that, but perhaps it was what she needed to hear.

***

One day, while Euphemia was getting ready to go to work in the morning, she got the news that turned her life upside down. She had just put on her uniform and was about to have her breakfast. It was unexpected that anyone from Kenya would be calling.

Ring. Ring—

Who is it? Euphemia thought and glanced at her phone. Her eyes landed on the caller ID, and she realized it was Ezra. She hurriedly picked up the call.

"Hello, Ezra!" Euphemia greeted him.

"Sis!" Ezra exclaimed. "Sis…Mom!"

"What?" she asked, worried. "What happened?"

"W-we managed to…we took mom to hospital last night, and she's not doing well."

"What? What are you talking about? She was well the last I conversed with her."

Euphemia's heart started beating fast, and she had trouble breathing.

"Ezra…can you please—please let me talk to her?" Euphemia told him.

"But Sis…," Ezra trailed off, unsure.

"Please!" she pleaded. "I just want to hear how she's breathing."

In the background, Euphemia could hear the sound that she knew all too well working as a nurse. She had heard this sound over and over in hospitals as she cared for dying patients, to hear it from her mother was fearful. It made her anxious and her heart was racing. Euphemia feared for the worst. She knew that her mother was struggling to breathe and guessed what might have been going on in that hospital room.

"Put the phone to her, Ezra!" Euphemia

Chapter 13

shrieked.

"Let me hear how she's breathing, please!" Euphemia knew her mother's life was fading right as she listened. She was scared for Almasi. It was her instinct that told her that her mother could be taking her last breath of life.

Euphemia cried; as her mother was struggling to breath, and she wasn't there beside her. She was helpless. There was nothing she could do as she was miles and miles away.

She heard Ezra communicating with someone, to then learn that it was a nurse. Ezra was attempting to get Euphemia closer to Almasi. Euphemia knew that her mother could continue listening in and maybe just say a few words that her mother could hear. Hearing and feeling are probably the last of the senses to go when someone is dying.

"We cannot let her talk to your mother," Euphemia heard the nurse say. "In this position, I fear it could be difficult."

And suddenly, she heard what she had dreaded—Almasi's groaning and agonizing voice.

"E-e-Ezra…Ezra!" Euphemia called out.

"Wait, Sis!" Ezra told her. "There is an emergency here. They need me right now. I will—I will call you back."

"What! Wait, Ezra—"

The call was hung up, and Euphemia couldn't do anything but stare at the phone. Placing the phone on the counter, she gazed at the walls in her kitchen dazed. She didn't know how long she sat there, she continued waiting for Ezra to call her back.

Ring. Ring—

"Ezra! What happened? Where did you go off to? Is mom okay? Can I—"

"She is no more, Sis!" Ezra cried. "Mo-om she has l-l-eft us-ss."

"What?" Euphemia replied as her voice faded out.

"She passed away a few minutes ago."

The phone slid from Euphemia's hand in shock. She remained standing near the kitchen island, unable to hold or do anything. She felt like a sharp knife had slit her belly.

Tears began to fall from her eyes, one by one, and then they constantly flowed. Placing her palm on her mouth, Euphemia tried to stop herself from screaming. She slid down the wall, sat on the floor and screamed out aloud.

She continued to scream and sob as there was no one in the house—she was alone. Euphemia felt the walls

Chapter 13

closing in on her. She felt suffocated, as if someone was choking her. She couldn't believe that the time she had dreaded most in her life, had come. There is a piece of her life that had just been taken.

Almasi died at the age of seventy-one, leaving behind a legacy of an empowering woman, men, and grandchildren who all loved her. She was not only a strong woman but a loyal wife and loving mother. Her sudden demise was soul-crushing for her loved ones—especially her children.

Chapter 14 – Is it Goodbye, Or see you Again!

"I know for certain that we never lose the people we love, even to death. They continue to participate in every act, thought, and decision we make. Their love leaves an indelible imprint in our memories. We find comfort in knowing that our lives have been enriched by having shared their love."
~ Leo Buscaglia

No one is ever ready for the aftermath after a loved one dies. Nobody wants to lose a loved one— it is definitely something no one wishes to happen unless them dying can release them from more pain. The hardest thing is the process we are forced to go through after their death. And one of the painful things is grieving and moving on from their demise.

An individual has to be strong and take courage to continue moving forward in their lives. It may take time to comprehend and acknowledge their thoughts and

Chapter 14

emotions after receiving that dreaded news-—that maybe challenging but also crucial to start the grieving process. One of the most important things in life is to embrace and cherish every moment of our lives and times spent with those we love. Remembering all the memories we create with our loved ones is a key to life. After they leave, they can open a door to exit but the memories will forever remain with us.

***

Within two days, Euphemia got on a flight to Kenya to go and give her mother her final sendoff and goodbye. Even though her family's financial status was very low and dwindled from the fact that she had been sending money to her family for her mother's upkeep. It was imperative that Euphemia had to travel to Kenya. It was a very heartbreaking feeling for Thabiti and their children because they were not able to attend the funeral due to the expense.

Euphemia and her husband could not afford to buy flight tickets for the whole family as the tickets were so expensive. Throughout everything, Thabiti supported her and told her, "Don't worry about the children or anything else, Euphemia; I will look after them. You just concentrate on paying the last farewell to your mother."

With a heavy heart, Euphemia arrived back in her hometown. She arrived in the city and had to take another flight to her hometown. She arrived late at night and her youngest sibling picked her up from the airport. The Airport was in the same town where her mother's hospital was and where her body lay in the mortuary. Euphemia requested her brother to drive her to the mortuary even though it was closed.

The sight was sad, Euphemia was unconsolable. Having her mother pass away while she was out of the country was even more devastating because she was a nurse. She cared for patients every day in America, while her own mother lay sick and later died being cared for by other nurses. She could not understand how she was great at her job and seemingly failed to serve her own mother. Life was funny that way sometimes, wasn't it?

After leaving the mortuary, they embarked on a few minutes drive to their home. As plans were being made to lay Almasi to rest, the family hosted several fundraisers to help raise funds from other extended family members. Euphemia and her siblings learnt their father's intention was to bury their mother in a non-traditional way.

He planned to place her in an isolated burial ground away from their house and near the farm by a banana plantation, out of sight so to speak. In the Barasa clan traditions, it would basically mean that Baraza can have another wife move into the home. It also meant that Euphemia and her siblings would not be able to live in the home as they had done before.

It meant that all the memories they had built living in the home would fade or be erased. It was painful for Almasi's children to imagine that their father would even think of perpetrating such an act. They wondered if he cared about them at all because he continued to

Chapter 14

torment their mother even in her death.

It could be accepted he didn't act lovingly towards their mother although very difficult, but to try and erase her legacy was shameful. She had sued him to keep her grounds and ensure that her children would have something from all her labor. Now, their father is wasting no time to erase that judgment and their inheritance. Euphemia was frustrated and heartbroken about how all these events were playing out. How can a husband treat his wife that way? How can a father treat his children this way?

Euphemia assumed from conversations with her mother, prior to her falling too sick, Almasi had given up hope because she was taking chemo medicine and was in so much pain. The whole process was agonizing for Almasi; the tests and treatment took a toll on her. And in her old age, it wasn't easy to cope with everything. Anyone could have thrown the towel in considering her circumstances; Almasi's strong will and heart simply succumbed.

Low and behold, as Euphemia and her siblings were cleaning up the house they found something that piqued their interest. They went through their mother's belongings, in the effort to try and preserve memories by keeping documents, pictures, clothes and many other things. Then they stumbled upon medication that had been prescribed to their mother. Their mom had never opened the medicines and they laid sealed, seemingly untouched.

"Why are they...," Ivy trailed off. "Why are they untouched, Sis?"

"I guess," Euphemia started saying. "Mom never took the medicines."

"What?" Ezra exclaimed, startled. "But why? Why would she do that?"

"She was tired." Euphemia swallowed. "It must have been hard for her to endure all her pain with no help of medication; she had been fighting alone all this time." She glanced at her siblings' sorrowful faces and said, "No one was there for her, especially dad. And we all know no matter what, mom loved dad with all her heart. His negligence and ignorance regarding her illness was not something anyone could reasonably understand. I guess—I guess she lost hope that anything would get better and she gave up."

"But—but mother had been painting and decorating the house!" the youngest, Zion, shrieked. "I thought she was trying to get well, so why did she let go? What was the reason behind all this! I cannot understand it!"

"No, no." Ivy shook her head, crying. "She wasn't decorating the house because she wanted to live again, but—but she was preparing for her death!"

"Ivy is right." Euphemia agreed, sighing. "We had completely misinterpreted her actions."

"If only we would've known earlier," Ezra mum-

Chapter 14

bled.

Yes, if only we had known, Euphemia thought. We could've talked her out of it. Alas! Little did we know she was preparing for her death.

Almasi had started preparing for her death, she had always been a woman that prepared and planned everything she had done. From family, finances, her children's education, and so forth she planned everything. And whenever she set her mind to do something, she accomplished it.

The preparation for her death was no different. Almasi never let herself get embarrassed, it was one thing she tried to avoid. To avoid embarrassment she became an incredible planner. She was always so meticulously clean and she taught her children to be the same way. Every morning when she woke up she showered and dressed up even when she wasn't going to work. The house and homestead always had to be cleaned and well kept. She ensured that her home was well maintained by assigning duties to her children and all her employees.

So likewise she did not want her visitors coming to lay her to rest, finding her homestead unkempt, so she cleaned and decorated it before she died. And boy did she do it! As her children reflected, she had spoken in passing many times through conversations as a joke about her desires for when she died. But who would believe that she was serious especially when it is your mother talking about her death?

Who really takes anyone serious when they talk about death? We all avoid the conversation as if not talking about it means it will not happen. On days like this, we remember that isn't true. Anyhow, the house was renovated and painted. The compound, the grounds all were cut and done, even the flowers were planted, gardened, and done!

Euphemia's sibling told her that the day Almasi died, she wasn't feeling well. She was having trouble breathing and consistently telling them how painful it was. For Euphemia, just listening to her mother's suffering pained her. She regretted not being with her mother in her last days and when she died.

It was late at night when Ivy told Euphemia that she had visited their mother, Almasi and she had told her everything. At that time, Ivy thought that her mother wasn't serious, so she didn't take her words into regards. Now, she wished she had written things down and taken her words into deeper consideration.

No child would want to hear about their mother's death! "What did she say, Ivy?" Euphemia asked her sister.

"She had requested, 'You need to give me a really good shower dress me in a white dress.'" Ivy replied.

"Mom—mom knew she wasn't going to see another day." Euphemia sighed. "That's why she wore a white dress to the hospital that day, isn't it?" Ivy nodded. The siblings stayed in their mother's room and cried

Chapter 14

about their loss that night. A piece of their heart had been taken away. They knew no one would ever love them the way she did. It was painful!

***

While filling out the hospital's documents, Euphemia recalled the past incidents. She remembered when her mother fell sick one night, and they took her to the hospital the following morning.

When Almasi got very ill, and unable to breath that night she was taken to hospital, before she died the following day. Ezra, Almasi's son had reached out to one of Alamasi's co-wifes, to come and help take her to the Hospital since Almasi and her children did not own a car. She was kind enough to help Ezra with transportation to the Hospital.

I suppose people come together in a time of grief and sorrow, Euphemia thought, smiling faintly. However, her smile diminished as soon as she remembered actions previous and present leading to some of the reasons their family was in the state and predicaments they were in. Even though it had been years leading to this specific time and period, Almas's pain lingered throughout the years. she had suffered a deeper blow with each new wife and how each one and their children were put before her own.

Throughout the time Almasi was admitted, Barasa never visited the hospital. He didn't bother to come to see his dying wife either. Or even visit the mortuary where her dead body lay. Euphemia knew very well that it was what her mother looked forward to. A small token of affection from her husband, but what she got in return was disregard.

Ezra continued, "When mother was taken to hospital that night, I called dad but he said there was nothing he could do, so there was not any reason he needed to come to the hospital" But the following morning after she had passed on, he saw his father. It was shocking to see him standing there in the hospital.

Barasa had never been there for Almasi. However, he was there seconds after she had taken her last breath, how ironic. It disappointed Euphemia how Barasa was never there for Almasi during all this time and had mistreated her all her life. He didn't visit her while she lived but only came as it appeared to confirm her death.

How absurd!

Ring. Ring—

The loud shrill of the ringtone propelled Euphemia to come out of her reverie. She glanced down at her phone and checked the caller ID.

Thabiti.

"Hey!" Euphemia said pleasantly.

Even though she didn't tell him, her husband still heard the sadness behind her voice.

Chapter 14

"Hello, darling!" Thabiti said with as much affection as he could to let her know she wasn't alone in her difficult time. "I know it's useless to ask this, but I was getting worried." A pause. "How-how are you doing?"
"I am…I am fine, Thabiti."

Thabiti sighed, knowing very well she wasn't. "Euph, if you need anything, please let me know," he told her. "And I am really sorry I couldn't be there with you."
"No, no, please don't," she commented. "It's not your fault, so please don't blame yourself."

"Okay." A pause. "How's—how's everything going?"

"There are some complications that my siblings and I are trying to resolve."

"What type of complications?"

"Father, he…he is throwing tantrums about mother's burial."

"Oh my God! What are you going to do now, Euph?"

"We are all trying to do our best. I hope we can bury her without any problems."

"Don't worry, you will."

***

There was a rule in Euphemia's village that if a man wanted a woman to stay in the house of his deceased wife, then he should not have the body of his deceased wife brought into that house.

Euphemia and her siblings had learned that their father wanted one of his youngest wives, their stepmother, to inherit and live in Almasi's house. Their house, a place they had called home all their life. Barasa never wanted Almasi's body to come back into the place like everyone did traditionally in their culture. He wanted Almasi to be buried further away in the banana plantation.

The siblings were furious; they didn't know how to handle this situation. They were angry that their father was willing to go this far. Nevertheless, Euphemia and her siblings still decided to fight for where Almasi was going to be buried and whether they could take her body back into the house. Euphemia's maternal family was enraged; they were not willing to take any more crap from Barasa "Do you think it won't matter where she will be buried because she's dead?" asked her Family.

Furthermore, "What and how does that reflect on her children that you're leaving behind? Or that you have already left behind?"

Euphemia and her siblings saw their uncle's and relatives on their mother's side arguing and fighting for their mother's rights.

"This is not going to happen! There is no way you're going to treat her on her deathbed the same way you treated her when she was alive." said her uncle.

Chapter 14

Almasi's family started making plans and arrangements for her burial and ordered for her casket. Euphemia and her sister Ivy got some flowers and other things that were necessary for the burial. It was around ten o'clock at night before they returned home.

Among the siblings, Euphemia was the one fortunate enough to be able to assist with finances and help out with the burial ceremony. Her brothers, sister, and maternal family had tried to pitch in to help them as best as they were able to.

Unfortunately, Euphemia's mother's eulogy was also written without consulting with her children, It was written by Alamasi's step children. It was then published in the daily newspaper without a true reflection and consideration as to what her own children would have really wanted to see written about their mother.

Euphemia made sure everything was according to what her mother had wanted for the ceremony. She looked for flowers her mother had loved. She wanted to give Almasi a proper sendoff, from this world she had called home for the eternity that God had given. She was hoping just maybe even though dead, her spirit would have some peace, she thought and hoped. Also, she wanted her and her siblings to have some satisfaction of having given their mother a good sendoff.

During Almasi's illness, her second born Baraka, was not around as much because he wanted to build a legacy for his family. So he really never got to see or witness any of her grief. Being the eldest, Baraka had to become a force to reckon with coming to the protection and fighting for his mother and siblings. Baraka had left his home country to find a better opportunity in another country. He hoped and wanted to work and help build a better life for him and his family.

He was referred and selected by a recruitment process to go work in an undisclosed location for security reasons on a contract basis. As his mother was dying, he was working a contract and could not break. Euphemia felt sad for him even more, because he wasn't able to get away like her, and her other siblings could. For him to return home to take care of matters was a touching act of love.

Almasi was in incredible pain, but even during this time she was concerned about protecting her children. She was worried about Baraka, not to the point where it stressed her out, but it pushed her to pray for him often. Baraka never thought he would lose his mother; he was barely aware of her condition. He wasn't able to see his mother when she was ailing for almost two to three years.

Being away was the hardest thing he had to do because he knew he was his family's protector; he was tall, strong, masculine, and desired to be a covering for his family. And Barasa knew that if Baraka came back for his mother's ceremony and burial, then he wouldn't let him do whatever he was planning. Barasa knew very well that push come to shove it would end into a bloodbath if his mother was not given the right to be buried appropriately.

Chapter 14

When the news got to Baraka about his mother's death, he was heartbroken. He regretted not being there with his mother in her last days. He asked for permission to leave so he could participate in his mother's burial. However, he was denied. Seeing him distressed and mourning for his mother, some of his colleagues took pity on him and helped him with an escape plan.

Baraka had to escape going over electrical wires to get out. Talking of dedication to getting what someone wants at all costs, he was the poster child. It just shows how much giving a last sendoff to his mother meant to him. Even if he got to lay an eye on Almasi's casket, that would be enough for him. Baraka kept telling himself, "I just want to see my mom. I know I can be victimized or arrested. Even if they arrest me and take me back, it's fine. I will be happy with whatever happens as long as I have seen my mother one last time!"

Baraka was more than aware that he could get arrested and sent back. However, he couldn't let this stop him from attending his mother's burial. He traveled overnight and arrived the night before his Mother would be buried.

The day of the burial was filled with the normal traditions—singing, dancing, rejoicing, crying, and wailing—the usual burial occurrences in their village. At night around eleven o'clock, Baraka arrived, and everyone was happy and sad at the same time to see him considering the reason. No one had seen him for many years so they were grateful to hug him and to bring the family closer. Baraka was overcome with happiness that he could pay his final respect to his mother and sad because he had missed everything during her illness. It was tragic that the last time he would remember seeing his mother, she was dead in a casket oh how painful it was.

In Barasa's culture the grave is usually dug at night, fortunately Almasi's children were blessed and her younger brother's In-laws volunteered to help. They had made up their mind to help Euphemia and her siblings bury their mother the right way. While Barasa was nowhere around, he had never visited the home, not even at this time to help console his children that had lost their mother.

His brothers went to the home to ensure Alamasi's grave was dug within the homestead as it should be. The two of them did not leave until it was done. They agreed with her children and her wishes, Almasi's body should not be laid to rest in the banana plantation, away from what she had built and called home for several years.

Barasa worked up a scheme of his own to ensure that Baraka Alamasi's eldest son never made his way to reach the home to bury his mother. He didn't want Baraka to be there because if he was, Barasa could not bury Almasi away from the house; his plan would be ruined, and he didn't want that to happen!

The next morning was like a battle day for Euphemia, her siblings, as well as Almasi's family. When they all were preparing to start events leading up to their mother's burial, including getting her body out of the house, they saw police officers in plain clothes coming toward

Chapter 14

the house. Euphemia and her siblings were then informed by well wishers that the police officers were there to take Baraka back.

"Euphemia!" Euphemia's uncle called out. "Find Baraka and go with him. Get him away from here as far as you can."

"What?" Euphemia shouted. "But what about you?"

"We will take care of everything," another relative told her.

"But—but!"

"Run along, Euphemia!" her uncle shouted. "We will handle the police officers. Find Baraka and get going. After we distract them, we will send word for you to come back."

Euphemia turned around and glanced at her brother. With one firm nod from her, she and Baraka began running toward the banana plantation and several hectares of maize plantation. Euphemia was barefooted and as she ran, she was being stuck by thorns, rocks pressed onto her foot, and insects stung her. The plants were also painful as she brushed up against the sharp edges of the plant. Baraka was still dressed in the same clothes he had worn the night before; he didn't get the time to change.

The siblings ran away from the house and ended up on a railway track shielded or rather covered by several hectares of maize plantation where no one would see them. They saw a public transport motorcycle and Baraka got onto a motorcycle and away he went. Euphemia and Baraka were running knowing that today was the day they were supposed to lay their mother to rest and yet they were on the run.

Euphemia and Baraka had gotten word from neighbors who sympathized with their position. They knew Almasi and wanted to see her keep her land and her children receive what was theirs. They worked as scouts and told them when it was safe for them to move about.

The neighbors told Euphemia and Baraka that the police were relentless, and it so happened that they had been tipped off by Barasa. He would turn in his own child for a new wife! How saddening this man kept proving to be. He was so dead set on Baraka never being involved in laying his mother to rest or his children getting their land, that he turned his back on his own son!

Euphemia came back to the homestead alone. Her heart was racing thinking about her brother. Baraka, distraught, had to go, unsure how he was going to get back to his work, and of the consequences awaiting him. To make matters worse, he was not able to lay his mother to rest as planned. Euphemia worried about him all night as well as the others.

Back at Almasi's house, the other children and grandchildren were equally worried about Euphemia and

Chapter 14

Baraka. Sitting quietly in one room, some were crying silently, tears were rolling down their cheeks as other grandchildren played oblivious to the serious circumstance. Yet Barasa and his side of the family were waiting to make a decision and proceed with the funeral without waiting on Alamasi's children to be present.

Almasi's body was prepared, the casket was covered and moved from the house to an outside tent all without her children participating or being present. When Euphemia came back she gathered her siblings, nieces, and nephews to dress up in a hurry and head to the ceremony. All the guests and the church were already seated.

When a mother dies, her children usually walk behind the casket as the body is removed from the house to go outside, but Almasi's children never got to do so. So what happened is they just went to the living room where her body lay last in the house, were prayed for by the church and then they were accompanied by the church and some relatives and walked to see their mothers' body in the casket laying in a tent outside before they went to sit down. All so tearful, so many thoughts going through their minds unbearably distraught and inconsolable.

Alamasi's children and grandchildren were the last people to sit down in the burial ceremony because they had to go shower and dress. They were the last to arrive after everyone else in their mother's burial ceremony also. If the emotions were not so high, it would have been even more devastating.

After going through a lot of pain and struggle, Euphemia, her siblings, and her maternal family were finally able to bury Almasi. It was agonizing for Euphemia to watch someone she loved leaving her. And knowing that she would never be able to see her again; It pained her. However, Euphemia remained strong throughout the whole ceremony for her siblings. Baraka, Ezra, Ivy, and especially Zion relied on her. They found comfort and support from each other.

Euphemia watched her father leave the ceremony quietly before her mother was buried. She was relieved that whatever her father had planned did not happen as he wanted. She and her siblings had finally given their mother a proper burial; and her father respecting that was the least he could do.

Chapter 14

Chapter 15 – Time Heals All Wounds

"You will lose someone you can't live without, and your heart will be badly broken, and the bad news is that you will never completely get over the loss of your beloved. But this is also the good news. They live forever in your broken heart that doesn't seal back up. And you come through. It's like having a broken leg that never heals perfectly — that still hurts when the weather gets cold, but you learn to dance with the limp."
~ Anne Lamott

The period of loss and grief that occurs after the loss of a parent can differ for everyone. Losing somebody we adore can be one of the most painful experiences we will ever want to go through. The fact that it's an unavoidable aspect of life is not arguable because at some point we all lose someone we love.

The loss of a loved one can be devastating, be it a good friend, spouse, parent, or child. The intensity and

Chapter 15

difficulty of the emotions we go through may come occasionally or frequently. These emotions could range from deep regret, loneliness, and anguish to surprise, loss of feeling, remorse, or sorrow.

However, what we need to know is that with every darkness, there is light at the end. If our life is filled with darkness right now, it will one day be brightened. We must never give up but continue each day to move forward with our lives.

People who have left us will forever stay with us—in our hearts and memories. Instead of suffering, we shall honor those moments we spent with them and move ahead with our lives.

***

It had been months since Almasi's death, and Euphemia had since returned to America to continue her life. She longed to get back to her loving husband and children. The hole that was in her heart missed her mother normally from being far away, and seemed to enlarge as she worked to accept her mother was gone.

It was hard to comprehend for Euphemia as she had never lost someone so close and dear to her before. She never thought that one day her mother's refreshing voice would completely vanish forever. She missed her dearly and felt helpless to change her emotional state.

Euphemia was going through a tough phase at that time. Not only was she longing for her mother, but she was also working through her guilt. She began to feel guilty for leaving her mother alone and moving to America. She thought about whether she was a good daughter or not. The truth of her being absent as her mother battled cancer plagued her heart. Her mother was always there for her, but when she needed Euphemia the most, she was gone. To make matters worse she was a nurse that couldn't–didn't nurse her own mother.

There is no other plausible explanation, Euphemia thought, gazing outside the window. I am a terrible daughter, she thought.

Euphemia couldn't forget the pain and trouble her mother went through. It would always remain in that deep part of her mind and kept rearing itself from time to time in her thoughts. Anytime she would think about her childhood and reflect on how Barasa treated her mother, herself, and siblings, she would get angry.

Euphemia sighed and glanced down at her lap. She stared at the photos of her childhood house and her mother's vibrant smile. Slowly—as if her hands could touch her mother's face—Euphemia ran her hands down the side of her mother's face.

She missed her mother! More than she could ever express or say! Nothing could contain the love she had for her mother.

Almasi was her world, the person who had shown her what strength, love, and humility were. Euphemia had always seen her mother fighting for her rights and standing up for herself. She had learned valuable lessons

Chapter 15

from her that she now almost always taps into.

Almasi was not only her mother but Euphemia's best friend as well!

Euphemia had observed her mother do so many things throughout the time they shared. She remembers how her mother prepared different foods and worked hard, but she regretted not asking her mother about her life in detail growing up. Almasi was a brilliant soul; she was an expert at many things. Euphemia wished she had known all of her mother's expertise, skills, and interest. She wanted to learn more from her mother—not only cooking and life lessons to pass down to her children.

Now sitting near the window in her house, Euphemia was trying to sew a torn dress hem in dim lighting. She imagined her mother's face, sitting beside her and smiling at her daughter's failed attempts. She had never been good at sewing although she knew it was an ideal skill her mother had. She often stuck herself with a needle because she made the wrong stitch. Almasi would often jump in to help her daughter finish the job.

As Euphemia remembered her mother she let the tears silently flow down her cheeks. Her mother wasn't here any more to give her a helping hand and it hurt so badly. She released all the emotions that had been building up for months and let them escape freely.

***

Even months after her mother's death, it seemed like yesterday that she had died in Euphemia's heart. One day,

when Euphemia returned home from work, exhausted, she was surprised to find an extremely nice letter waiting for her on the living room table. With beautiful flowers beside it, she picked it up and thought
What the…? Who could they be from and why? Euphemia opened up the note and said within her mind,. Oh my God! It's Thabiti's writing! Euphemia was pleasantly surprised; she didn't know why and when her husband planned this but she was grateful. She began reading the letter.

"'Hey, Honey!"

I know you have gone through so much in the past few months. Your mother's death was heart-wrenching. She took a part of our hearts with her leaving some voids that can never be filled.

Darling, I cannot express how it pains me to see you like this. You and the kids are my world, and It hurts me to see you hurt.

Love, take as much time as you need to grieve. Just know that the children and I will forever be there for you. You have our support and love. Meanwhile, here is why I cherish and love you with my whole heart.
You are my wife and closest friend. You never give up on anything, please don't give up on this."

You allow me the space I need and help me in my difficult times.

Every day, you make me laugh.

Chapter 15

I am honored that I fell in love with a stunning woman Inside and out.

You understand me for who I am.
I don't think I know anybody more compassionate than you.

You have a lovely voice. It soothes me whenever I hear you solve problems.

Even though you have gone through so much, you still remain optimistic about life.

Everything about you makes me want to do anything for you to bring the smile back to your hurting soul.
" I love you, Euphemia!"

The tears flowed from Euphemia's eyes overwhelmed with emotions. She couldn't believe that God had blessed her with a loving husband. He did not just understand her distress but was also willing to be present.

Euphemia had always thought that maybe it was her mother's prayer that she found Thabiti.

Instantly, Euphemia folded the letter neatly and pushed it inside her pocket. She glanced at the time; it was eight in the evening. He must be at home! She began her search to find her husband. Euphemia rummaged from one room to another but could not find him. Where is he? Euphemia was distressed. Is he late? He had never been this late, so why isn't he—

A loud, happy laughter broke her train of thought. Euphemia gazed around the living room, confused because she didn't know where the laughter was coming from. In an instant, her eyes found the backdoor, and she realized the voice was coming from there. Taking a deep breath, Euphemia began walking toward the garden.

A picturesque view greeted her sight when she opened the door. It brought warmth and comfort into her heart. Euphemia leaned against the door and watched Thabiti, Faraja, and Bahati planting seeds across the side of the lawn and laughing. Having fun together.

"Mom!" "Mommy!" her children cried out.

Faraja and Bahati came running up to her as soon as they saw her. It caught Thabiti's attention too, and he turned around to stare at his wife. He smiled at them embracing each other.

"Mom! Come on!" Bahati shrieked. "Play with us, please!"

"Uh…," Euphemia trailed off, not knowing what to do. She glanced at her husband and saw him nodding his head silently. "A-alright."

The children screamed and jumped in joy. Euphemia walked to where they were and sat beside Thabiti on the floor. For the next few minutes, the couple watched their children plant seeds into their garden.

Chapter 15

"Thank you for the flowers and beautiful expression of a letter," Euphemia muttered, turning to gaze at Thabiti.

"Hmm," Thabiti hummed and then shrugged. "You're welcome, darling."

"You know I feel blessed to be your wife," she mumbled, laying her head on his shoulder.

"Really?" he asked, playfully surprised. "I think I am blessed to be your husband."

"How about we both are?" says Euphemia to him.

"That, honey, is very true!" he gently said to his wife. The couple laughs aloud, finding joy and pleasure in their moment.

"How—how are you feeling right now?" he asked her.

"I am good, thanks to you," she muttered.

"I am delighted to know I can be the reason behind it." Tabiti says with a grin.

"You are, honey." She closed her eyes. "You are."

The couple quietly listened to the birds chirping and their children's laughter. It was a peaceful and comfortable environment for them.

"Hey, I want to tell you something!" Euphemia exclaimed, lifting her head from his shoulder.

"What is it, my sweetheart?" Thabiti questioned, worried and tensed.

"I love you, Thabiti!" she mumbled, gazing and smiling fondly at him.

"I love you, too, Euphemia!" he murmured, grinning back at her. He began to lean toward her—expressing his love with a slow and passionate kiss.

***

Days passed into months, and months turned into years, and Euphemia's wounds healed with the time passing. The pain of losing her mother had somehow lessened—it was still there, but it hurt less. She made a habit of praying for her family, siblings, and Almasi daily like how her mother had done.

It was what made her fridge ahead with life. It was difficult for Euphemia to get her life back on track for some odd years. However, things slowly started returning to normal, and she was content. She fought hard to make her life blissful and happy again.

Along with Thabiti, Faraja, Bahati, and Euphemia embarked on a journey to find themselves. Euphemia's goal was to share the love, lessons, and freedom her mother gave her with her family. She wanted them to be free to live, love, and make mistakes in peace. This perfect love her mother gave her, she wanted to be perfect with

Chapter 15

her family also!

Chapter 16 – Shame, Guilt, Regret

"The only things I regret, and the only things I'll ever regret are things I didn't do. In the end, that's what we mourn. The paths we didn't take. The people we didn't touch."
~ Scott Spencer

It was a difficult time for Euphemia dealing with the pain of losing her mother. It can be suspected that the regret she felt was because she wasn't there. Often she thought about how children grow up using their parents for everything, then one day they leave.

She never understood the sacrifice her mother gave although she empathized. She knew there was nothing she didn't do for her growing up and even when she became an adult. It was hard to return to the states and see her children and family ready to welcome her. She knew that warm welcome would never reach her mother again, and in that moment she felt ashamed.

Chapter 16

As she sat down with her husband one afternoon looking into the backyard. She had no focus point but her attention was drifting any which way the wind blew on this sunny cozy day. Her husband gently sat next to her and didn't say a word for several moments.

She acknowledged his presence but was still locked in a trance, caught up in her thoughts. He placed his hand on her leg and said, "Do you mind if I continue to sit here with you?"

She tenderly responds, "No honey, I don't mind that you are here."

"You look so deep in thought, do you want to talk to me about it?" her caring husband asked.

"I don't know why these gushes of emotions seem to sweep over me. I know I will have to adjust but I am not ready. But I don't have a choice. I feel like I never got the chance to say goodbye. To show her my children, my family, her family."

She continued on to say, "I just have so many regrets on how I lived my years concerning my mom. I wished I would have involved her more in our lives, is all."

Thabiti, took a pause before answering. "Your mom was a powerful woman who understood you. She raised you and knew what you needed at times more than you. She never disliked that we moved to America. She knew the sacrifice you would both have to make."

The only things I regret, and the only things I'll ever regret are things I didn't do. In the end, that's what we mourn. The paths we didn't take. The people we didn't touch

"You are being hard on yourself, Euphemia and death can make us do that. Lost, grief can show the tender parts of us. But knowing that these are your raw emotions and not the truth about our situation points you in the right direction to grieve our loss." He said. "You are the best thing that happened to me and our children. Your mother is a great part of that. I know you feel like our children do not know her, but every day they see she is inside of you. Death doesn't mean we forget those we love, but we keep them alive by the lessons they have taught us and the future we intend on making."

This wasn't the first and only conversation Euphemia and her husband had to have concerning her mother's death. The truth is death causes all of us to grieve differently. She wasn't the only one impacted by the death of her mother.

It took weeks to see how much her mother had impacted her children and husband. Being close to someone that you love and grew up with while others have not, can make you feel like you are grieving all alone. Her children didn't spend years living with their grandmother but they have heard the stories of her life, and their grandmother.

They were all aware of the love, faith, and hard work their grandmother had done for them. Euphemia wanted to be sure the warmness she felt in her heart to-

Chapter 16

wards her mother would never die. She wanted it to also love on in her children. She remembered the Bible lessons her mother taught effortlessly and how she wanted to give that to her children.

For many years Euphemia struggled with the death of her mom on and off, but her mom dying didn't make her think to connect with her father. The relationship with her father had always been estranged. Surprisingly, her father had met her husband many years ago, but there was no attempt to connect his grandchildren with him.

Travel expenses were partly responsible, logistics, but desire also played a role. Euphemia never thought she would desire to have her children spend quality time with her father. Even after the death of her mother, the love and attention was not transferred to her father. However, something else was. Living in the United States gave Euphemia and her family the ability to support her family financially. Throughout her mother's sickness she was contributing to expenses and making sure her brothers and family had what they needed to care for her. She felt great to be able to provide that help, but always wanted to be there to care for her also. However, with her father, to her surprise, she committed her heart to be there for him during his darkest hour.

Chapter 17 – Forgiveness

Because forgiveness is like this: "A room can be dark because you have closed the windows, you've closed the curtains. But the sun is shining outside, and the air is fresh outside. In order to get that fresh air, you have to get up and open the window and draw the curtains apart."
~ Desmond Tutu

If there was ever a time in my life where I could sympathize and understand my mother's love for him, it was then. When Euphemia's younger brother sat in the room with him one day he made a confession. He said, "Of all my children, you four are the only ones who were raised right. I should have spent more time with your mother. It is a shame what you see when you get old that you can't see when you are young. Don't wait until your eyes are cloudy to see clearly."

Chapter 17

Perhaps Euphemia's mother saw his regret long before he would realize it. Maybe her connection with God the Father showed her that someday he would get what she was working to create, a home for them all. Her passion was to provide a safe place and inheritance for her children.

Euphemia was sure that deep down inside, she wanted her and their father to connect on raising their children. She didn't want them to grow up the way they did, and had hope they wouldn't leave this earth without seeing him differently.

Euphemia once recalled talking to her husband and saying, "I really don't understand him. He was so cruel to us growing up. Do you think he means any of this or is afraid of death?"

Her husband responded, "I think death makes any man think and consider his ways. If there was ever a time to make amends and get things right, surely death will make a point of it. Is this not what your mother prayed for you to think?"

Euphemia had never considered what her mother prayed for. She knew that she prayed without ceasing and that her prayers worked. She is a living testament of her mother's prayers. But she never knew what she prayed for her father.

"You think my mother's prayers are still working even beyond the grave?" she asked her husband.
"I see no reason why they wouldn't. I am so grateful to

have met your father and get his blessing, meant something to me. I know it meant something to you too."

"Yeah, that day was so... shocking. My father had hardly acknowledged me over my lifetime. You saw him at the funeral. Hard to see that man as the same guy from many years ago or even now. I never understood my father."

"Do you think you should try to get to know him more? This is the last time you may have to find out your questions and get some answers. Doesn't the father tell us to forgive? Euphemia you have a beautiful heart, look at what you are doing for your father–a man who you said never cared for you. You are a wonderful daughter."

"Thank you honey. I am not sure how to start a conversation with him. But you are right, I should try."

"Maybe I can help you rehearse it? If your dad was right here, what would you want to ask him?"

"Okay, Dad...dad, how come you never spent time with us? Why did you treat my mother the way you did? What did she do to you that made you feel you couldn't love her? How come you treated your own son like that at her funeral? Why did you never give her peace even though she tried to do that for you?"

Euphemia started to cry as she spoke and her husband embraced her. He held her for several moments after she spoke and as she sobbed on his shoulder she began to feel released. For the first time, she considered

Chapter 17

asking the questions to her father that she never could with her mother alive. Maybe, just maybe she could get some answers for why her mother treated him so well when he treated her so poorly.

Although the conversation was in her heart and mind to have with her father, Euphemia never built the courage to ask. She would see him on video or hear his voice and couldn't bring herself to ask. As she saw her dad pass away a little at a time, she began to understand her mother more. She realized her mother was teaching her a lesson she could only get by seeing.

Her mother was teaching her long suffering. She was teaching her unconditional love. She was affirming what we should do for family and how God can love unlovable people sometimes. She wasn't sure if her husband had accepted faith, but she wanted him to. She wanted to exemplify Christ so he would know who Jesus was. In his latter days he looked on how my mother treated him and her treatment was the greatest witness that Jesus lives.

She did what no pastor could do for him because he wouldn't allow it, she lived as a living sacrifice set aside for God's use. She bore a heavy load and withstood judgment, rejection, pain, and at times shame. She was not deterred and never turned her back on her promise to God. It was never about her father but always about her commitment to God.

When Euphemia's mother made a vow, she hardly broke it. She would pull off crazy mandates, learn anything she could to provide for her children, workers, or family. She had a given heart and she gave it to her husband as well. She gave to all his wives and their children too.

Although Euphemia was not close to her step children, they all knew who her mother was and many had a place for her in their hearts if they cared to admit it. Many told me after her funeral how impactful she was on their lives. They were grateful to her and wanted to tell us so.

Euphemia had never been close to her step siblings. They hardly played together or did much than taunt them wherever they could. Almasi's children were all the black sheeps of the family. It wasn't until their father passed away that they reached out more and apologized for how they had treated them growing up. Euphemia forgave them as well as their siblings, but the bond didn't grow much after; mutual respect only forged.

Of all the families he had chosen to build, it was my mother's family that provided for him financially and how he requested in his latter days. Mother was still given to everyone beyond the grave and Euphemia finally got it when her father passed away. She realized that family isn't perfect but they are there to help cultivate aspects of your character.

No one gets patience from opening a box, but from being conditioned through experience, heartache, or pain. It was hard for Euphemia and her siblings to love their father, but they did not disappoint God or their mother in his last days. They let him live in peace and

Chapter 17

helped him to rest easy.

Ephemia gave God all the praise as she laid her father to rest, seeing that he could change anybody if they would only surrender to Him. Her father would have never admitted that he made a mistake but he did tell her brother he regretted calling the authorities on him at his mother's funeral. He tried in his own way to make up for that. God was always the glue that held the family together and it took all the moments and prayers for this to be evident to Euphemia and perhaps to you as well.

"No matter where you may be, how badly someone has messed up, God can change your life or that person's life. No one is too far away from the healing hand of Christ Jesus. Be encouraged by my words and share this story with as many people as you meet. By hearing each other's testimonies we all overcome."

About the Author

"What you won't do for a stranger or someone you dislike, shows your character. Everyone should love those who love you, but it is those who first love you that make all the difference!"
~ Effie Rubia

Effie Rubia, "saved by grace, living by faith," grew up in Kenya, as a first-born child. Initially focusing on education and field hockey, Effie attended foundational education in Kenya. Her mom wanted the very best for her and her siblings, so she attending boarding school including Nursery school.

Effie respected education and even upon coming to the United States, furthered her career by attending two more Universities in America. She's the wife of a rock star husband, the mother of three exceptional young adults, and a handsome prince of a grandson. She moved to America in the early 2000s and currently lives in the

About the Author

countryside of Georgia with her husband, two of her children, as well as "the dog" and the "the cat."

Living in the countryside has helped her overcome amaxophobia and nyctophobia she developed during her early childhood. Today, she enjoys working in the medical field, writing, and spending time with her family, often taking long drives and star gazing. Currently, Effie has one book published, The Extreme Odds Endured and intends to explore publishing more books.

www.ingramcontent.com/pod-product-compliance
Lightning Source LLC
Chambersburg PA
CBHW062038120526
44592CB00035B/1268